Praise for Bill

MW00678955

5

The Steve Spurrier Story:

"Chastain brings to life the man behind the myth in this fascinating and intimate portrait of America's most controversial coach."

—Matthew Brzezinski, *The New York Times Magazine*

"There are no Switzerlands when it comes to Steve Spurrier. Neutrality gets the score run up on it. You love him or hate him. Chastain's book helps us with the hard part: understanding him."

—Martin Fennelly, *Tampa Tribune*

Payne at Pinehurst:

"As you read[*Payne at Pinehurst*], my hope is that you too will be inspired by this recollection of the 1999 United States Open, and that you will be stirred by the accounts of a man who inspired me daily, my husband, Payne Stewart."

—Tracey Stewart

Steel Dynasty: The Team that Changed the NFL:

"Chastain does the obligatory personality profiles of players from that era and the book has many interesting and funny anecdotes. However, where the book really takes on a different bent is when Chastain delves into the innovative coaching strategies employed by Chuck Noll and defensive coordinator Bud Carson. Noll is an intensely private man and has rarely given a glimpse into his coaching genius. However, Noll explains the methods to the Steelers' success in this book and Carson, who died earlier this month, shows how he molded the defensive schemes to the strengths of their players. Chastain's recounting of how the Steelers completely stifled the Minnesota Vikings to win their first Super Bowl is must reading for anyone interested in the strategic intricacies of football. Yet, he explains it in such plain language that even casual fans can understand the thinking behind the moves. Chastain also does an outstanding job of illustrating how the Steelers' success changed the NFL forever."

—John Perrotto, *Beaver County Times*

Peachtree Corvette Club:

"As a newspaper guy, Chastain always excelled when it came to feature writing, as opposed to covering a beat. That's not a knock, it's just a fact. Details and subtleties were his strength, and once again he puts his powers of observation and nuanced writing to good use in *Peachtree Corvette Club.*
—Bob D'Angelo, *Tampa Tribune*

The Streak:

"Former *Tampa Tribune* baseball writer Bill Chastain shows his appreciation and passion for baseball's past and present with a fast-paced novel that embodies elements of *Bang the Drum Slowly*, *The Natural*, and even *Ball Four*."
—Joel Poiley, *Baseball America*

SEPTEMBER
NIGHTS

SEPTEMBER NIGHTS

Hunting the Beasts of the American League East

James Shields

Pitcher, Tampa Bay Rays

as told to Bill Chastain

cadent PUBLISHING

Printed in the United States of America

ISBN 9781937644000 (pbk.)
ISBN 9781937644017 (eBook)

Cover and interior design by Janet Robbins, North Wind Design & Production, www.nwdpbooks.com

Cover photo credit: Thomas Northcut
Interior photo credits: Author's collection; baseball by Tage Olsin

Cadent Publishing
9 Gleason Street
Thomaston, ME 04861
www.cadentpublishing.com

Contents

Foreword

We had a special group of players on the 2010 Tampa Bay Rays, and that group had a mission: to win the American League East division and return to the World Series.

A lot of people didn't expect us to contend in 2010 because of the division we play in, which has always been dominated by the Yankees and Red Sox. Many baseball fans seemed to think that the 2008 season should have had an asterisk by it since the lowly Tampa Bay Rays won the division that year. I think a lot of us on the team carried chips on our shoulders for that reason. We were the ugly stepchild of the A.L. East.

After a disappointing 2009 season, we reported to spring training in 2010 with the idea that we would do whatever we had to do to get back to the top spot. At the beginning of September, we found ourselves right there with the Yankees. What unfolded next is the story told in *September Nights*.

James Shields, my teammate and friend, has worked with Bill Chastain to write an entertaining account of what happened down the stretch. Any reader will know a lot more about baseball and a lot more about the players who played for the 2010 Rays after reading *September Nights*.

Our ownership did an outstanding job in 2010 of putting the guys in the clubhouse we needed to win. Not only did they create a talented team, they also assembled a team that had the right chemistry to win. We won, and we had fun while we were winning.

The 2010 clubhouse was awesome, and we have a similar clubhouse in 2011. We have a lot of guys who get along. It's fun to interact with everybody on the team. You can approach anybody at any time. That's the way I felt last year, and it's the way I feel this year. It's a special feeling. Honestly, the feeling is a lot like the one I got when I played at Vanderbilt University. Some of the guys on our team went to college, and some of them didn't. Those who did can probably tell you that this is a college atmosphere, with everybody getting along and hanging out, on and off the field. There aren't a lot of teams that can say that.

As the 2010 season unfolded, we all knew we had a finite window of time to get the thing done together. We knew it was probably the last time that core group of guys—including 'Los, C.C., Soriano, Bartlett, Garza—would be playing together. We wanted to make it work, and we did.

Those were exciting and special times for a special group. *September Nights* captures the thoughts, emotions, and highs and lows of a stretch run by a team pursuing destiny.

—*David Price*
August 2011

INTRODUCTION

WE WERE PLAYING IN DETROIT during the 2010 season when Bill Chastain approached me about writing a book with him detailing the final month of the season. From the outset, the idea interested me on a couple of fronts. First, I was intrigued about the process of completing a book. Though I wasn't aware of how much work takes place before you reach the final product, I knew I wanted to be a hands-on guy where the work was concerned. Second, I thought baseball fans would like to hear the story of our team as seen through the eyes of one of its starting pitchers. So I agreed to take part, which led to plenty of time spent with Bill, answering his many questions and filling his recorder with anecdotes about my career, the Rays, and events taking place during the final month of the 2010 season.

We have strived to capture the story from an insider's point of view. Being that insider, I tried to be as forthcoming as possible about how we conducted our business on the Tampa Bay Rays while trying to win our second American League East title in three seasons. *September Nights* provides insights about life in the major leagues, including behind-the-scenes impressions of opposing players as well as impressions of the characters who were my teammates on the 2010 team. In addition, I offer a lot of information about what I'm trying to do when I'm out there on the mound, which I believe might be of interest to any fan of the game. And hopefully I have fully conveyed the bond that we had on that team, a bond that grew stronger from enduring the earlier "Devil Rays" era, when we were the joke of baseball. We had lost a lot of games together before growing up to become winners in baseball's toughest division.

Midway through the 2010 season, we all understood that our time together as a team was growing short, because our management planned to cut payroll prior to the 2011 season. That knowledge created extra tension. We knew that this group of guys was using its last chance to reach our goal of winning another division title. If we could accomplish that goal, we'd have a chance to progress to the World Series once again, and this time, hopefully, win.

I enjoyed working with Bill on the project. Once *September Nights* was completed, I especially enjoyed reading what we had created and reliving the memories from that special season.

—James Shields
August 2011

Changeup

ONE
August 29, 2010

SEPTEMBER NIGHTS HOLD MAGIC for any team lucky enough to be in contention for the final act of the season.

I've experienced those nights, and now, in 2010, I can again look forward to what the nights will bring once the calendar reaches the ninth month of the year.

When I first reached the major leagues with the Tampa Bay Devil Rays in 2006, any suggestion that our club would be fighting the Yankees for the American League pennant would have been met with a laugh track suitable for a celebrity roast. But change happens, and I've been fortunate to be a part of the transformation from "Devil Rays" to "Rays"—a profound occurrence that has seen a perennial loser become American League East champions in 2008 and contenders to win the toughest division in baseball for a second time in 2010.

I'm James Shields, right-handed pitcher, and I'll always remember the Devil Rays, a team known for wearing green, playing in a funny building, and losing a lot. We lost 101 games in 2006 and finished 36 games out of first place. The guys wearing the pinstripes finished first and beat us 13 times in 18 games that year.

Flash forward to last night, Sunday, August 29, 2010.

Tampa Bay's team is no longer the "Devil Rays"; we are now known as the "Rays." We don't wear green anymore, and losing is no longer a part of our culture. Those changes took place prior to the 2008 season, when we came from nowhere to win the American League East and advanced through the playoffs to the World Series before losing to the Phillies.

By this time in 2006, guys would already have begun planning hunting trips, golf outings, and exotic vacations for the second the season finished. Now it's all about baseball. Nobody's even mentioned the off-season. Last night, the guys in the dugout cheered every pitch I threw against the Red Sox. Offsetting those cheers were anxious glances at the scoreboard to see what the Yankees were doing. Scoreboard watching at Tropicana Field—go figure.

A loyal following of 23,328 attended the Sunday night game, which was shown on ESPN. Pitching in that kind of setting is why you play the game. Yes, making a lot of money to play the game is pretty sweet, too. But moments like last night make all the hard work worthwhile.

I have struggled this season. I feel like I'm riding a big roller coaster, climbing the heights of quality starts and plunging to the drastic lows of pitching what I would consider some horrendous games. I began the season with a 5–1 record and a 3.08 ERA in my first nine starts. After May 25, my season kind of tanked. This whole second half, I've really dedicated myself to getting back to where I need to be when I take the mound.

If you're a pitcher and you're losing, you tend to analyze everything. You fight the tendency to look back on what happened in your last outing, but sometimes it's hard not to do that. I know I have to get back on track and stay on track. I've given up a lot of home runs. The truth is, I'm always going to give up home runs because I throw strikes. My pitches are always going to be around the zone. That's one of the secrets to logging over 200 innings every season. I like to have the other team put the ball in play. Who wouldn't mind having the ball in play while pitching for this team? Since June 22, we've only made twenty errors in sixty games, which is two fewer than any other club in the major leagues and ten fewer than the next closest team in the American League, the Yankees. Unfortunately, one of the by-products of putting the baseball in the zone is the possibility that a hitter will square one up. And believe me, they've squared up a few against me this season.

Saturday night I sat at home with my parents and my wife. When the conversation came around to Sunday's start, I told them that I viewed the start as one of the biggest games I would pitch all year. I felt a lot of pressure going into that game. I knew I needed to step up my performance for the team and that I couldn't worry about my numbers, even though they aren't the kind of numbers I want hanging on the back of my baseball card. My mission in the start would be to keep the score close. We haven't been scoring a lot of runs, so keeping the Red Sox from scoring runs meant everything, particularly with John Lackey scheduled to start for the Red Sox. He had been pretty tough on our guys in the past.

You are going to feel a lot of extra pressure anytime you face the Yankees or the Red Sox. Both teams have a lot of professional hitters who know how to work counts to their advantage. They'll spit on any pitch outside the strike zone and foul off the strikes they don't like. Facing that kind of hitter can elevate your pitch count in a hurry, which is what they want to do. The quicker they can get the starter out of the game and start getting after the bullpen, the better their chances of winning become. You feel a lot of pressure knowing you'll be dealing with hitters like that.

On top of that, a major league strike zone is small. They've definitely minimized the width. I remember watching baseball games as a kid. Guys like Greg Maddux would get two, three, four inches off the plate and still get strike calls. That's just how the strike zone was back then—wider and shorter. Now it's skinnier and taller.

Going into the game, I had a goal of trying to throw just one or two different pitches early in the game. I have four pitches: fastball, curve, changeup, and cutter. My fastball is just a straight fastball. My cutter looks like a fastball but has a little bit of a cut to the left. It's a pitch that I've really developed, and it's been pretty good. It keeps hitters from really sitting on the fastball. I'm looking to miss the square part of the barrel with my cutter. Ideally, the hitter will pop it up or ground out early in the count. It's not a strikeout pitch for me. I might throw a backdoor cutter to a left-handed batter or frontdoor cutter to a right-handed batter to get the occasional strikeout. I try to nip the back outside corner of the plate with the backdoor cutter against the lefty, hoping he'll think the pitch is outside and give up on it. And I try to catch the front inside corner of the plate against a righty, hoping he'll think the pitch is inside and maybe even jackknife away from it.

But for the most part, at the beginning of the game, I didn't want to show all my weapons. There are just too many good hitters on that team. I knew if I showed them everything early, my pitches wouldn't be effective later in the game. And things turned out as I hoped they would. Later in the game I started using the curveball a lot more because they were sitting on my change. When I gave them a different look with the curveball, they had a hard time making good contact. I had a lot of swings and misses and a lot of takes for strikes because they didn't recognize my curve from their previous two at-bats against me.

Marco Scutaro personifies the kind of players you face anytime you pitch against the Red Sox. He signed a two-year deal with Boston back in December. Before signing with Boston, he played for the Blue Jays. He's a good player, and he knows how to work an at-bat.

He led off Sunday's game for the Red Sox, and when he stepped in there, I'm on the mound thinking, "This guy has statued me 0–2." When a hitter "statues" a pitcher, you know from the way he's just standing there that he's going to take the pitch, and it ticks off a pitcher big-time when a hitter does that and you throw him a ball. A lot of times a hitter will statue you on the first pitch just to see what you have. With Scutaro, you don't know when he's going to statue you. He's done it to me before and I've thrown him a ball, and I've gotten so mad I wanted to hit him—I just wanted to hit him. But that's the kind of hitter he is. He's scrappy and a really good guy to have hitting in the leadoff spot. I think he's become one of the best leadoff hitters in baseball over the last couple of years, and he's a grinder.

In the first inning Sunday night, I had Scutaro 2–2. Then he fouled off three straight pitches, and I'm thinking to myself, "Not this early in the game. I don't want a hundred foul-offs." Next thing you know, your pitch count is 30 and it's still the first inning. So when Scutaro grounded out to Jason Bartlett at shortstop on the eighth pitch, I felt a lot better and told myself, "Now that I got him out, I can get down to business." I wanted to be aggressive to finish out the inning, so I threw a steady diet of fastballs down to J.D. Drew and Victor Martinez. Three pitches did the job against Drew, and I got Martinez on the first pitch, so I felt pretty good about the first inning.

I call the first inning the "amp inning." You're so amped up to get the game started that sometimes you don't know what's going on. When you get done with the first inning, the game usually slows down a little. Pitchers and coaches always say your game is going to be dictated by how you pitch the first. If your first inning goes well, you can start settling in and getting a feel for things. If it goes bad, you'll probably have to grind out your remaining innings.

Over the past several years, the Red Sox have been a huge rival. I guess that mostly stems back to 2008, when we went back and forth all season before we finally won the division. They've had some turnover since then. Manny Ramirez got traded before the 2008 season was over. Jason Bay went to the Mets. But they brought in guys like Martinez and Adrian Beltre, and they still have their regulars like David Ortiz, Kevin Youkilis, and Dustin Pedroia. Unfortunately for the Red Sox, they've had more than their normal share of injuries this season. At one time or another this season, they've lost Jason Varitek, Josh Beckett, Clay Buchholz, Jacoby Ellsbury, and Mike Cameron. In addition, they lost Pedroia early in the season due to a broken left foot. That injury didn't heal properly, so he had to shut it down for good when he tried to return. Earlier this month they lost Youkilis for the season when he needed surgery to repair an injured right thumb. Amazingly—thanks to their depth—the Red Sox have managed to stay in the race.

All of the guys who are playing in place of the injured have good approaches at the plate. You'd like to take them lightly, but you can't—even a guy like Yamaico Navarro, who was playing second base on Sunday. He looked at strike three his first time at bat, but his next time up, I threw him a fastball and didn't focus enough on making my pitch. He hit it back through the middle for a single that drove in a run.

Navarro's single scored one in the fifth, and Scutaro singled home another to put the Red Sox up 2–1. Beltre doubled with one out in the sixth and scored on Daniel Nava's single to right field to push the lead to 3–1. We answered with three runs in the bottom of the sixth to take a 4–3 lead.

I pitched 6 ⅔ innings and struck out eight to come away a 5–3 winner. Our bullpen came in and cleaned up, with Randy Choate and Joaquin Benoit getting us to the ninth, and our closer, Rafael Soriano, getting the final three outs to pick up his thirty-ninth save of the season.

A funny element about my situation is that I'm the old man around here, and I'm only 28. The franchise doesn't have a lot of history—Tampa Bay's first season was 1998, and, like I said, they experienced a lot of losing in the past. So there still aren't a lot of milestones and records worthy of mention. My win gave me 56 for my career, making me the franchise's all-time leader in wins, and the start gave me 145, also the most in franchise history. Neither is exactly an epic mark, but reaching them means a lot to me. The Tampa Bay organization has given me an opportunity to pitch in the majors, and hopefully I'll get a lot more starts here in the coming years. Doing the math, at the rate of 56 wins in five years, if I play another 25 years I should be knocking on the door for 300—*right*.

Speaking of franchise marks, Carl Crawford hit the one-hundredth home run of his career during Sunday's game, which moved him past Fred McGriff into third place on the Rays all-time list for home runs in a Rays uniform.

To tell you how special a player C.C. is, think about this. He's the eighth player since 1900 to reach 100 home runs, 100 triples, and 400 stolen bases. At 29 years and 24 days old, Crawford reached the 100/100/400 milestone younger than anyone in major league history. In fact, he reached it almost four years younger than the previous youngest, Lou Brock (32 years, 11 months, 11 days).

C.C. is unique. He's really strong—his hundredth home run traveled 420 feet—and he's amazingly fast, whether stealing a base or making the outfield look small because of all the ground he covers. If you put him in tights he'd look like some kind of superhero.

Carlos Pena, who holds the distinction of being the top dog on the list of top home run hitters in the Rays' history, also homered in the game, giving him 25 for the season.

Dan Johnson got the winning hit for the second night in a row with a bases-loaded single. That guy's amazing. It seems like every time they call him up from the minor leagues, he comes through in the clutch. Johnson hit a walk-off homer in the tenth the night before to give us a 3–2 win over the Red Sox.

Those are the kinds of games we win, the one-run and two-run games. Our team always seems to find a way to come to life in the late innings and score runs. We usually get a quality start from our starting pitchers, and then the bullpen comes through by holding them in the end.

Beating the Red Sox in Sunday's game gave us 10 wins in 15 tries against them this season, which means we only have three more games against them, since we play all of the teams in the East 18 times. That's a good thing, because we always have to battle them like we do the Yankees.

Going into our weekend battle with the Red Sox, I felt like it was the biggest series of the year for us. If they had swept us, they would have been just 2½ games behind us. The fact that we took two out of three meant they boarded their plane for their next series in Baltimore trailing us by 6½ games. If they want to get back in the race, they will have to somehow pull off a 14–game swing with a month left in the season, and that's really hard to do. I want to feel like we put away the Red Sox this weekend. If we can go out and continue to play our game and just try to win each new series, we might have put them away. But you can't write those guys off. Even though the Red Sox have a big job in front of them, they aren't going away. That's the American League East. We have the best division in baseball. It's going to be disappointing at the end of the season when one of the teams with one of the top four records in baseball doesn't go to the playoffs. But I love this division, and this is where I want to be.

We now have an 80–50 record, keeping us in a tie with the Yankees for first place in our division with two games left in August before the calendar flips to September.

The ninth month of the year can be magical or dreary in the major leagues. Every kid dreams of experiencing what we did in 2008. I know it sounds clichéd, but it's true—going to the post-season makes you feel like a little kid again. Once you get there, it's not about you anymore. It's about the team and the feeling, the magnitude, of the world watching you. You get butterflies in your stomach. During the season, you get eager, but you don't get nervous. But going into September, knowing you're in the hunt is pretty special.

Last year ended up being pretty disappointing. We had a good team. In a lot of areas we were actually a better team in 2009 than we were in 2008. Things just didn't break the right way for us last year. We got off to a slow start and had to play catch-up ball all season. At the beginning of last season, it didn't feel like we had the vibe. Halfway through the season, we definitely had the vibe, but by then it was too late. That's what the Red Sox are dealing with right now. April was a terrible month for them, and we had a good one. We understood the importance of starting out well in April. Starting out well gave us the opportunity to be where we are right now. After we played our way into the postseason in 2008 by winning the American League East, not making the playoffs in 2009 really hurt—I mean, really hurt. If I had never experienced the magic in 2008, not making the playoffs in 2009 might not have hurt so much. But we did experience the magic in 2008, so what happened in 2009 crushed us.

Our manager, Joe Maddon, really focused on our slow start in 2009 and how we could avoid getting off to a slow start in 2010. It seemed like all we talked about during spring training was getting off to a good start. And that's exactly what we did. We went 17–6 to start the season, including a streak that saw us win nine out of ten on our first road trip. Since then we've had some struggles here and there, but we built up a lot of equity before we experienced any kind of real trouble. Now we're in the hunt heading into September. All is well right now for the most part. We know we've got just as good a chance to win the division as the Yankees. So we'll ride all the emotions of the game during the coming month—complete with scoreboard watching and butterflies. The Boston series definitely had a playoff atmosphere. We were in the dugout on the edge of our seats every single inning. That's what it's going to be like for the next month. You can't hide from it. Instead, you have to embrace it. Save for my wife and kids, it's all I'll think about until we're eliminated or win it all. It's going to be on my mind every day. I'd be lying if I said it wouldn't be. It's almost surreal, because you work so hard during the off-season and during spring training with the goal of making the playoffs and World Series and here we are, on track to have a chance to do just that.

In the ten years I've been in the Rays organization, I've experienced seven losing seasons. That's why a lot of teams in baseball—and fans as well—still have a hard time seeing us at the top of the standings, as if the whole thing is a fluke. But talking to other players around the league and listening to what they have to say about us, I know we are respected by our peers. Having said that, I'm sure the Yankees are wondering why we won't go away this season. Their team is supposed to win. Their players are the premier players in the league. They are the defending champions. They've got a $200-million payroll and we have a $72–million payroll. Nevertheless, I think it's been seven straight games that we've been tied with the Yankees for first place. I'm sure the guys in their clubhouse are watching our games on the scoreboard, and we're watching theirs. That only adds to the excitement. We'll just keep grinding it out.

We're not a big-market franchise, which means Rays fans are going to see a lot of guys coming in and going out. Andrew Friedman does a phenomenal job of bringing the right guys in. Signing a guy like Benoit is a great example. He had right-shoulder surgery and missed all of the 2009 season. Nobody knew how that would turn out, but Andrew and the guys running our team felt he was worth the risk. We have an unbelievable training staff to take care of all that stuff. And everything that went into trading for Soriano was brilliant. Andrew had traded Akinori Iwamura to the Pirates for Jesse Chavez, which worked out nicely because the Rays weren't going to keep Aki anyway and he would have become a free agent. When Soriano unexpectedly decided to forego free agency and accept arbitration, the Braves didn't want to go to arbitration with him. So Andrew traded Chavez to the Braves for Soriano and signed him to a one-year deal. Andrew does a great job of bringing the right guys in, and we end up winning every year.

In the backdrop of everything good that's going on for us there hovers a closing window of opportunity. Nobody on the team really wants to talk about it, but everybody knows that our team will not be the same next season. We play in a "small market," and that means we cannot pay Crawford what he'll get on the free-agent market. Soriano, Benoit, and Pena are probably in the same boat as well. We love playing together on this team, so the feeling is bittersweet that we won't be together next year. This is one of the odd situations you get put into in baseball. We play together as one. We want everyone to succeed. And, above all else, we want to win together. It gets weird when you have to factor in that you're an adult and you have a chance to set up yourself and your family for generations to come with the money you might make by taking the free-agent route. If you're a grown man and you have an opportunity to sign that deal, you've got to sign it. Still, that's a tough decision, because it goes against all the reasons you have always played sports: to be a part of a team, a unit that works together to achieve something together. While that perceived window of opportunity for us to win a World Series appears to be closing, we won't truly know until next season who will be here and who won't. In the meantime, all we can do—and what we want to do in our hearts—is to go for it, to give everything we have for the remainder of the season while we try to defy the odds by claiming our second American League East title in three years. We've got the players on the field that we feel can win the World Series. We know that the team's management plans to drop the payroll next year. But things can happen. Things can change, and you never know what or how. We can't control that as players. We just have to keep going out there and doing what we do. We can't control what the ownership decides to do. We don't know if we're going to lose half our team next year. What we do know is that we're in first place right now, and our goal is to win the division and the World Series. Why not take care of business before that window of opportunity slams shut?

Standings on August 30

Tm	W	L	GB
TBR	81	50	--
NYY	81	50	--
BOS	74	57	7.0
TOR	68	63	13.0
BAL	48	83	33.0

Curveball

TWO
August 30–
September 1

W HEN WE WERE IN THE 2008 PLAYOFFS, I caught a lot of crap from the national media once they got wind of my nickname "Big Game James." They asked, "When has he ever pitched in a big game?"

Well, I had to agree with them. The moniker never really fit, but it wasn't like I gave that name to myself. We all know there's only one "Big Game James," and that's James Worthy, who was the man when he played for the Los Angeles Lakers. Believe me I know that, having grown up in the Los Angeles area. Worthy was my all-time favorite basketball player.

But everybody gets a nickname in the minor leagues, and getting mine was just one of those things. Chris Flinn, a guy I played with in the minors, hung it on me. Your nickname doesn't matter in the minor leagues, since nobody pays attention to you, but mine stuck when I got to the big leagues because a lot of guys in the organization had come up from the minors and were used to calling me that. What can you do? I just sort of went with it, even though I'm not the kind of guy who has a big enough ego to strut around as if I really am Big Game James. But next thing I knew, all the reporters were asking, "Why are they calling you Big Game?" Then we got to the World Series and I felt like the whole name thing got magnified by a million. Everybody who covered baseball was calling me that—you know, "Big Game James is on the mound"—and I'm sure a lot of them were thinking I was full of it. I couldn't stop that from happening, but having that nickname definitely put a little more pressure on me. Over the course of my career, I feel like I've pitched pretty well. I can definitely hold my own, but I'm not one of the superstar pitchers in the league, and I'm not going to be the guy going around calling myself "Big Game" either.

Nicknames sometimes evolve to other nicknames. Last year mine made the transition to "Juego Grande," which is "Big Game" in Spanish. Then Pat Burrell shortened it to "Juego G." He told me, "You're not 'Big Game James.' You're 'Juego G.'" Now everyone calls me "Juego G." Maybe if we make the playoffs this year, "Juego G" will get more of a ride.

So now it's Monday, August 30, and the Blue Jays are in town for three. Wade Davis pitches well in the first game of the series. He went on the disabled list with a right shoulder strain in early August, but ever since returning to the team he's been coming on strong. We win 6–2, and the game lasts just 2 hours and 15 minutes. Compared to the games we usually play against the Red Sox and Yankees—which seem to run anywhere from three to four hours—this game feels like it's still in the fifth inning when it ends.

Carlos Pena homers for the second night in a row, giving him 26 for the season. He's been having a tough season, but he continues to be a team leader. Good things really began to happen for the franchise when Carlos became a regular player during the 2007 season.

We still held spring training in St. Petersburg when Carlos came to camp in 2007. He'd signed a minor-league contract with an invitation to spring training, so he was at a crossroads in his career. He'd been a high draft pick and a major leaguer, yet here he was fighting to get a major-league job. We played our exhibition games at Al Lang Stadium, next to the bay, and most any hitter trying to make the team while playing in that park had to feel screwed. Talk about a graveyard for well-hit balls! Al Lang fit the description perfectly. The field had deep fences, and the wind always seemed to be blowing in. Carlos hit a lot of balls hard that spring, and he showed that he could be a selective hitter, but at the end of camp he didn't make the team.

Then Greg Norton hurt his knee. Norton was a good player, but his injury and subsequent knee surgery prompted the team to bring back Carlos. Given another opportunity, Pena turned around his career. He hit 46 homers that season and had 118 RBIs—both still club records—and he established himself as a team leader. Carlos cares about people and has a great disposition. Seeing him out there playing for us now, and knowing that he's a free agent after this season, makes me sad. It's hard to think about the Rays taking the field without him, but that's probably what's going to happen next season. That's just the business of baseball.

Jeff Niemann is over nasty when he's on the mound standing all of 6-foot-9! But right now Jeff and I are scuffling a bit. Jeff starts the second game of the Blue Jays series on August 31 and only allows one run through the first five innings. It looks like he might have straightened himself out until the sixth inning, when the Blue Jay bats get busy ringing up six runs on five hits. We lose the game 13–5 while the Yankees are busy beating the Athletics 9–3, which puts them a game up on us in the standings heading into the final month.

One thing few people outside baseball can understand is the daily pulse of the game. Losing badly to Toronto in the second game of the series probably looks like a dire situation to our fans. Some of the national TV shows point to the loss and come to the conclusion that the Yankees are getting ready to bury us. Inside the clubhouse, though, the feeling is different. When you play 162 games, you just can't get too upset after a loss. Joe Maddon always tells us to allow a half hour after every game to stew over a defeat or celebrate a victory—and then move on. For the most part, that's the way we operate. In this particular case, it is a lot easier to move on knowing we have David Price pitching tomorrow night. Who better to kick off the final month of the season than our best pitcher?

Desmond Jennings starts in right field on September 1. He just came up from Triple-A Durham, where he has established himself as the heir apparent to Carl Crawford in left field. You can't hear anything about the future of the Rays without hearing Desmond's name. He's really athletic and was accomplished enough as a wide receiver in high school that Alabama offered him a scholarship. Brad Hawpe starts as the designated hitter. Colorado just designated him for assignment, so we picked him up as a free agent. And Dioner Navarro starts at catcher. Navvy has had a tough time this season. He was supposed to split the catching with Kelly Shoppach, but he got suspended after getting ejected from a game early in the season. That's when John Jaso got recalled, and when Shoppach had to have knee surgery, Jaso stayed with us. After having some big games offensively, Jaso settled in as the starting catcher and Navvy ended up at Durham until his recent selection by the club. Jaso won the job with his bat.

Jaso is definitely one of our better hitters and has the best on-base percentage on the team. He's not afraid of anything and has a good eye at the plate. Give Joe credit for recognizing that fact and using him in the leadoff spot for much of the season. A catcher in the leadoff spot is a rare thing, but it's been working for us.

We all call Jaso "Mikey" because of something funny that happened the first time he got called up in 2008. Carlos Pena called Jaso up to sing on a bus ride and called him "Mike" Jaso instead of John. We all thought it was funny so we started calling him "Mikey" from then on.

Price allows one run and four hits in eight innings to pick up his sixteenth win of the season. Typical of Price, he keeps his fastball up in the 97 to 98 MPH range the entire game, which he's been doing all season. This is his fiftieth start in the majors and his twenty-sixth career win. Since 1952, only seven other pitchers have as many as 26 wins and 266 strikeouts and an ERA of 3.53 or lower in their first 50 starts. Roger Clemens was the last guy in the American League to have that kind of start to his career, so Price is in pretty lofty company.

A nice feature of entering September is the expanded roster. In addition to players being brought up from the minor leagues, extra coaches can dress out, too. So Don Zimmer, who has been a special advisor for the Rays for the last several years, has dressed out for Price's outing against the Blue Jays, which allows me to sit and talk to Zim for most of the game. What a thrill for me, not only to be watching Price pitching like he's been pitching, but to pick Zim's brain during the game. I get chills having Zim on the bench. I mean, this guy is a legend. He's never drawn a paycheck outside of baseball. He played with Jackie Robinson on the Brooklyn Dodgers. You don't normally get anybody on the bench who has been in the game as long as Zim. We're talking 63 years in baseball, and fortunately for me, I have enough perspective at this moment to want to take it all in. You've got to respect anybody who has been in the game as long as he has. I just want to interact with him and hopefully absorb some of his knowledge.

Everybody enjoys messing around with him during the game. He's 80 and old-school, but he's contemporary, too, and he knows the art of give-and-take when it comes to dealing the bull. It seems like he's laughing most of the game, and even when he isn't laughing he has an ear-to-ear grin. Of course, from a baseball lifer like him, what do you expect? No matter how much the game has changed, he still loves baseball. He can't disguise that fact.

Throughout the season, Zim has been in uniform before all of our home games and for some of the road games, but that's just before the game starts. Prior to September there's a set limit to the number of guys who can be in uniform on the bench, so he's had to change clothes before the game starts and either watch the game in the clubhouse or go home. Once I notice Zim on the bench for tonight's game, I say, "Zim, I didn't know you'd been called up." He says, "I'm on a one-day trial. You guys better win or else I'm outta here. Joe said if we don't win, I'm gone."

When Evan Longoria gets up to bat with Crawford on second, Zim turns to me and says, "I'll tell you a baseball phrase you've never heard before: 'Longo needs to pickle one here.'" I say, "What? 'Pickle one?' What does that mean?" He says, "It means he's got to hit one out," and then he starts going at it. "Come on Longo, let's pickle one." He hasn't said anything the whole game, but now he's excited because he's using one of his phrases from back in the day. I feel almost like I a time traveler back to Brooklyn's Ebbets Field in the 1950s. Zim's next to me on the bench and we're both wearing flannel uniforms and yelling for Pee Wee Reese to pickle one, and Jackie Robinson and Gil Hodges are next to us yelling the same thing. Nobody on our bench has ever heard anything about pickling one, but that doesn't stop Zim. The saying has been awakened in his mind, and he's more than tickled to use it.

Price pitches a gem in front of us, but he gets taken out after the eighth inning. He's allowed only a solo home run to John Buck in the fifth inning, but we've only scored once against Shaun Marcum. Price isn't too happy when he gets to the bench, because he's been taken out without a lead and may not get a win. Nobody wants to mess with Price when he's like that—except Zim.

Zim turns to me and says, "Dad-gum, he thinks he's so smart from Vandy, but he's the dumbest pitcher I know." I'm kind of taken aback, but Zim goes on, saying, "He's so dumb, he's mad that he got taken out. That idiot shouldn't have given up the homer and he'd be winning 1–0." I crack up, almost falling off the bench. I tell Zim he needs to tell Price what he just told me. He goes, "All right, I will."

When Price gets up, I say, "Hey Price, Zim wants to tell you something." Then Zim repeats what he told me, and Price loses it just like I did. He's all smiles after that. Zim tells me that when he managed he used to needle his pitching staff that way. "They knew I was serious, but they also knew I was joking," he says. Then he tells me that Price pitched a hell of a game and shouldn't be mad about anything.

Longoria singles in the bottom of the eighth to drive home Ben Zobrist to put us ahead 2–1. Then Rafael Soriano gets the final three outs to become the first pitcher in the major leagues to reach 40 saves, and Price gets the win.

Sean Rodriguez has supplied the rest of the offense, going three-for-three with a single, a triple, and his ninth homer of the season, leaving him a double away from hitting for the cycle.

Sean came to us last season in the trade that sent Scott Kazmir to the Angels. He has turned into a nice player. He's shown some pop in his first full season in the major leagues, and he can play a lot of positions—so he gives the team a lot of flexibility, and he's a good guy in the clubhouse. All of those are appealing elements to the guys who run the Rays. The current ownership group headed by Stuart Sternberg hasn't made too many mistakes. Andrew Friedman is our general manager, and he goes by the title of Executive Vice President of baseball operations. Call him what you will, he's a general manager, and a good one.

We've taken two out of three from the Blue Jays to start September, leaving us a game behind the Yankees with a record of 82–51. Just think about that. We're 31 games over .500 and only in second place. Doesn't seem right, does it? That's life in the American League East.

Prior to leaving for Baltimore after the Toronto series, we are all keeping an eye on Hurricane Earl, a Category 4 storm that appears to be headed toward the Mid-Atlantic states. According to all the weather forecasts, Baltimore sits in what they are calling a "medium-threat area." The worst-case scenario will see us in the middle of a hurricane on our off-day in Baltimore. At the very least, we are likely to have some rain delays or maybe even a rainout. With the season winding down, the weather is one of the unknown factors that can mess with a team. Pitching rotations can be affected, as well as the team's overall energy. Sitting around during rain delays or having to play a double-header to make up for a rainout can become hardships for a team to deal with during a season. It's just part of baseball.

Standings on September 1

Tm	W	L	GB
NYY	83	50	--
TBR	82	51	1.0
BOS	75	58	8.0
TOR	69	64	14.0
BAL	49	84	34.0

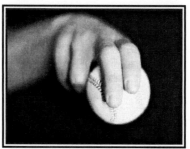
Two-seam fastball

THREE
September 2-3

Being a major league baseball player is everything it's cracked up to be, particularly when you get to be around guys like the other pitchers in our starting rotation. We have a lot of fun.

Between Matt Garza, David Price, and me, we're always getting on each other about stupid stuff. For instance, my hair is too long right now, and I've been putting gel on it. I didn't have a great June or July, so I decided to do a little something different, superstition-wise. When I got called up in '06 I had this big old Afro. I'm this white guy with curly hair, and everybody thinks I'm half Black because I have this Afro. After this season's All-Star break I decided I wasn't going to cut it, so that's where I'm at right now. Of course they all abuse me for it. In turn, I make fun of Price for his hair, or lack thereof. He's 25 years old and bald.

Price is a trip. Basically, he is the most competitive person I know except for myself. That makes messing with him a lot of fun, like the time I saw him sitting down on the bench stuffing bubble gum into his mouth. I couldn't resist getting something started, so I said, "Man, you've got a lot of bubble gum going, how many pieces have you got in there?" He said he had five. I sat down beside him. Knowing who he is and how competitive he is, I sneaked six pieces into my mouth. He's like, "Wow, you've got a lot of bubble gum in your mouth." I said, "Yeah, I've got six pieces in there. That's one more than you have."

Next thing you know, game on. He started unwrapping gum and loading up, probably figuring that would be that. Instead I kept pace with him. My mouth bulged, but I kept going. Eventually we each had 26 pieces of bubble gum in our mouths. We couldn't even chew because the wads were so big, but Price wouldn't stop. I knew he would keep going until he had one more piece than me. That's just how he's wired. When he shoved the twenty-seventh piece into his mouth, I decided to throw in the towel. He wasn't going to lose. That's just the way he is in anything he does.

I call Jeff Niemann and Wade Davis the silent assassins because they're not really outspoken, they are sneaky funny. You will be sitting there and next thing you know they will say something that will start cracking me up.

Garza and I are realistic about our situations and what might happen given the way the Rays do things. We understand that one or both of us might not be here next season given that we'll both be making decent money and the organization has another pitcher ready to make the jump to the majors. Jeremy Hellickson is that somebody.

Hellickson carved up Triple-A hitters this season before joining us in August. He led the International League with a 2.45 ERA while going 12–3 with 123 strikeouts and just 35 walks in 118 innings. He has the look of someone who is going to be special.

Helly made four starts with us during two separate stints with the club in August and became the first pitcher since 1920 to pitch six-plus innings, allowing three hits or fewer, in each of his first three major-league appearances. And he won his first three starts, which made him the only pitcher in club history to do so other than Joe Kennedy. Overall, he is 3–0 with a 2.05 ERA as a starter for us this season. Now, in September, he's back for his third stint with the team and will be pitching out of the bullpen.

Heading to the bullpen is not at all unusual for a young starter. Most young pitchers who come up from the minor leagues aren't physically used to pitching into September. That's something you have to build your body up to in your career. Pitching an extra month can damage the goods, so they'll use Helly some in the pen and ease him into the final month. That's what they did with Price in 2008, and he ended up really helping us.

Given Price's ability, of course, that wasn't a big surprise. Every Rays fan remembers him coming into Game 7 of the American League Championship Series against the Red Sox with the bases loaded and two out in the top of the eighth. Price used a filthy slider on the black to strike out J.D. Drew and end the inning, and he followed that up by getting the final three outs in the ninth, which got us into the World Series.

Going back and forth between starting and relieving isn't easy, though. I've always thought that the cool part about being in the bullpen would be the possibility of getting into any given game. As a reliever, every day when you arrive at the ballpark, you know there's a chance that your number will be called, so you stay ready. That's the fun part. The difficult part comes in getting up and getting ready in a short amount of time. A starter can take as much time as he wants to get ready for a game.

I'm sure they'll go easy on Helly, because they see him as being a piece of the rotation. And I have to agree with that opinion. He's a cool customer. When he's on the mound, nothing seems to rattle him. Everybody's already taken to calling him a flat-liner. He doesn't seem to have a pulse. That's a nice compliment for any pitcher to receive.

Hellickson's success has stirred up some of our fans, who would like to see him replace me in the rotation given the up-and-down year I've been having. I've seen that suggested in the media as well. It reminds me of a backup quarterback's situation. Fans always think the guy on the sidelines holding the clipboard should be calling the signals. After all, didn't he lead that memorable touchdown drive in the final exhibition game before the season? In this case, I'd say Helly is good enough to be a major-league starter right now. If this were the old days with the Devil Rays, he probably would have been with us last year.

But even if Helly might be a threat to my job, that doesn't

bother me. I plan to do all I can to help him. I definitely plan to ask him if there's anything I can help him with, and to see where he's at. I really like him. As a player you always think somebody's going to come up and take your job, and sooner or later that player is going to come along. Ultimately, helping a player isn't going to be what costs you your job, and helping someone is good karma. That's just the way I think about it because that's who I am. "Whatever goes around, comes around," I believe. Baseball has a family element to it. We're a small family, and everyone around the league should help each other. That's how I feel.

While I plan to help Hellickson all I can, I also plan to compete with him. I'll do all I can to keep my job. That's what competition is all about, and competition is just a part of playing a professional sport. You know there are guys like Hellickson who are coming up and want to take your job. I was that guy, and still am.

I've been the team's opening-day starter for the past three years, but I know next year that's probably going to change. Price came in here wanting to be the number-one starter. We're really good friends. We go out to dinner together. We hang out together. We play video games and do all kinds of stuff to keep our minds off baseball. We do everything together, but he wanted to take my job from the day he arrived. It didn't matter if he was my best friend or not. He wanted to take my job. I love that competition.

When I got called up to the Devil Rays, there were only a few pitchers around to show me the ropes. Additionally there were only a few of us on the team who went to the gym to work out on a regular basis, and I remember wondering if I was doing something wrong. One day in the gym, I half-jokingly asked our strength coach, Kevin Barr, "Is this what I'm supposed to do?" He said, "Yes, this is what you're supposed to do." Back then strength training wasn't a big part of the team. Luckily, my cousin Aaron Rowand had helped change the way I did things.

My mother and Aaron's mom are sisters. Aaron, who is 33, got to the major leagues as an outfielder with the Chicago White Sox in 2001, and I can never thank him enough for pointing me in the right direction long before I made it to the major leagues. His influence and instruction taught me the right way to go about my business.

After missing the entire 2002 minor-league season due to surgery on my right shoulder, I found myself looking for a way to get healthy again while also getting better conditioned than I had been in the past. If I couldn't get my shoulder right, getting to the major leagues would be out of the question. A lot of troubling thoughts can enter your head in the aftermath of surgery. You question whether you'll ever be able to rebound, which leads to questions about what you're going to do with your life if you can't. I had turned down a baseball scholarship offer from Louisiana State University to sign with the Devil Rays after they drafted me out of high school in the sixteenth round of the June 2000 draft. After getting injured, I had regrets about not having gone to college. At least I would have had a degree to fall back on if baseball didn't pan out.

I told Aaron I needed a place to work out, and he invited me to join him in Las Vegas for a month, so I did.

Heading out to Las Vegas, I didn't really know what I was going to do. I just knew I had to do something different with myself in order to get my career back on track. Vegas seemed like my only option at the time, even though, in retrospect, I'm sure there were other routes available. Prior to my first workout with Aaron, he told me they started at 6 A.M. He didn't say anything else. I told him, "Okay, I'll be there at six."

When I got to the gym at 6:01 A.M., Aaron and his workout partners were already lifting weights, and he told me to go home. I said, "What do you mean go home? I'm here, let's work out." But he said, "No, we don't show up at 6:01. We start lifting at 6 o'clock, and you might want to be here a little earlier than that to warm up." He was angry and added, "Don't embarrass me, go home." I said, "Are you serious?" He said, "Yeah, go on home. This is not the type of work ethic we have." After that I would be sleeping in my car in the parking lot outside the gym at 5:30 in the morning. A couple of times Aaron had to come out to the car and knock on the window to wake me up. Reed Johnson, who went up with Toronto for his first year in the majors in 2003, also worked out with us.

After a month of that, Aaron told me I needed to stay in Las Vegas, so I ended up renting a place and we worked out throughout the off-season.

Working out with my cousin was great, because it came at a time when I needed help the most. My future felt so uncertain at the time. My wife and I were together and living frugally off my

$200,000 signing bonus. I put some money into some investments, and we lived off that and the $200 weekly salary I received during the season. But there were no guarantees that I would be able to come back to baseball healthy enough to pitch.

Tim Soder was our trainer. He's a physical therapist, so I knew I was in good hands having him around to watch over my repaired rotator cuff and the nerve damage in the back of my shoulder. He did a bunch of tests on me the first day and was able to force my arm down with just two fingers. I had nothing back there, no strength at all; it was all gone. I had no muscle, and the nerve had seemingly died in the back of my shoulder. Tim tells me to this day that he didn't think I had a chance to throw a baseball again, but he didn't tell me that at the time, and I'm very glad he didn't. In my mind, I just knew everything would be fine and I'd continue to pitch.

I worked hard that off-season and ended up having a decent season at Single-A Bakersfield. Most importantly, I stayed healthy all year.

Getting used to the workouts we did served as a wake-up call. Until then I had no idea what working hard was. We concentrated on the core muscles, which involve the big muscles in your legs and butt. When I began working out with the group, I could hardly walk for three weeks. I literally could not sit on the toilet without my butt hurting. But I knew in the long run those workouts were going to pay off, and eventually they started getting easier and easier. I learned tolerance, and I learned how much weight I could lift. I progressed to the point of wanting to lift more than anybody else. When you're not sore and you're able to work out, it's actually kind of fun. Now working out is a part of my routine. If I miss an off-season workout, I don't feel like I've done anything with myself that day.

I can never repay Aaron for helping me the way he did. He pretty much taught me everything about how to do things, how to act professionally, and how to train the right way in order to keep my body in the shape it needs to be in to be a professional athlete. I give him a lot of the credit for the kind of work ethic I have today.

Life as a minor leaguer is never easy. My wife and I had our first daughter in August 2003. During the off-season, I would work out from 6 A.M. to 9:30 A.M., getting home soon enough to take care of the baby so my wife could get to work by 10 o'clock. Sometimes we look back and wonder how we did it, but having a kid turned out to be a blessing for us, because that experience changed our lives. I looked at things differently after that. Nothing was just about me anymore. A lot of guys who get drafted are all about themselves because they don't have any responsibilities. When you have a kid, you have responsibilities. It's about taking care of your family any way you can.

My wife and I went through a lot of stress during that period. There we were in our twenties with our first child, living on our modest incomes. But I think we're a lot stronger for struggling the way we did. We ate ramen noodles every day, twenty-five cents a bag, trying to fill up on that. Even boxes of cereal were too expensive. We laugh about it now, and I like to tell everyone how lucky we were to have a kid who loved eating ramen noodles for breakfast. Trying to be good parents, my wife and I had decided we were going to eat the ramen noodles ourselves but make sure our daughter ate well and could have whatever she wanted. But I asked her one time if she wanted cereal, and she said she wanted the noodles, so we were good with that. We weren't about to force that expensive cereal on her. The kid loved noodles, what can I say!

Adding to the pressure of the situation was the reality that the only thing I knew how to do was play baseball. Fortunately, I had a relentless attitude about me. I just had to succeed, and I didn't think twice about the possibility of not making the big leagues. Somehow I managed to keep all the doubts from entering my mind. I just tried to work as hard as I could and continued to hope for the best. Everybody knows the odds of making the big leagues are heavily weighted against you. Not only do you have to have the baseball skills, you also have to be lucky enough to stay healthy. Nevertheless, I had that kind of mentality that I was going to make the big leagues and nothing was going to stop me. The way I trained not only helped condition me but also gave me a lot of confidence that I would succeed. Feeling that way is important. My work ethic also helped shape the opinion the Devil Rays had of me, and they rewarded me accordingly.

After parts of two seasons in the majors, the Rays decided they liked the way I pitched and the way I prepared, so they signed me to a long-term deal early in the 2008 season. They wanted the organization to change its ways. They told me they wanted me to be a leader, and they wanted everyone to emulate my work ethic. And it's worked out pretty well for Price, Garza, Niemann, Davis, and me. We all get in there to work out. We have our routines. Busting our butts together seems to have been a successful way of doing things for us.

Fortunately we get to Baltimore without any problems from Hurricane Earl, which heads farther north, leaving us to deal with the Orioles and not the weather. We feel pretty good escaping any schedule problems.

After our day off in Baltimore, Garza starts against the Orioles on Friday night, September 3. Garza is really funny and helps keep the clubhouse loose. The only thing predictable about him is that he is unpredictable. You never know what he's going to do, though he does have his rituals. Eating Popeye's Chicken before his starts is one of the things you can count on. He'll buy a bunch of that fried chicken so anybody who wants some can join him. Also, he doesn't talk to reporters the day before one of his starts, which has frustrated more than one reporter. A lot of people might attribute that to Garz just being quirky, but it's become a part of his routine, and he follows his routine religiously because he believes that gives him a better chance to win.

Garza manages to stir things up a little prior to his start against the Orioles. Normally when the media talks to you before your start, you say things about finding your fastball command or keeping your pitch count down--nothing too inflammable. Not Garza. Ditching the usual dull pitcher rhetoric, Garza gets excited when the media asks him about his upcoming start in Baltimore. He obviously remembers the last time he pitched against them, and he still has a chip on his shoulder. Back on July 20 in Baltimore, the Orioles hit four home runs against him, two by Luke Scott and three by successive batters in the second inning of our 11-10 loss. So Garza tells the media: "They went back-to-back-to-back, and Luke Scott [hit two], so I'm going to make them feel really uncomfortable in the box."

Baltimore has been playing a lot better since Buck Showalter took over as their manager. He managed the Yankees and Rangers before going to ESPN for a while. With Showalter as the team's manager, they went 17-11 in August. Incredibly, that's the first month they've had a winning record since June 2008. Garza calls the Orioles a bunch of young guys who are out there to make a mess of everything. Being the competitor he is, he's intent on getting the best of the Orioles this time around. He adds, "You expect that from them. But I owe them a lot of payback for the type of outing I had last time against them."

Garza is Garza, but one thing you can count on—the stuff he throws really can make hitters look uncomfortable at the plate. Sometimes it seems like he can pitch with his fastball alone, and when you add some of his breaking stuff, look out! And to his credit, when he steps on the mound at Camden Yards, he backs up his mouth—sort of. He allows one earned run in 5 $\frac{2}{3}$ innings, and we win 4-1 to remain 1 $\frac{1}{2}$ games behind the Yankees. The Yankees have already won today, and we knew that before we played the game. But that's nothing new. We don't play any differently just because the Yankees won or lost. We just figure they're going to win every day, since that's what they always seem to do. You've got to focus on the things you can control, and that means playing the game the best we can. The Yankees are still in first, but we're not going anywhere.

Actually, Garza's performance proves to be a lesson in damage control. Some nights you don't have great stuff, other nights you have great stuff but can't harness it, and some nights you're just lights out and everything is working. But mostly, you're out there trying to find out what's going to work for you on this particular night. If you don't have your best stuff, or you get into trouble, you're looking to minimize the damage. That's what Garza does. Something else he does is go soft on fastball counts, using his change-up and curve when the Orioles hitters are looking fastball.

He gives up five hits and three walks. He also throws two wild pitches and allows base runners in every inning but the first. But like a true professional, he allows just the one run on a sacrifice fly to Felix Pie in the fourth. The Orioles go hitless in six at-bats with runners in scoring position, and yes, Garza has a little something to do with that.

Garza and Joe Maddon do a little verbal sparring when Joe takes him out. I know how Garza feels. He's frustrated, and he makes a remark that doesn't sit well with Joe. None of us likes getting taken out of a game. Garza thinks he has more left in the tank, and Joe understands that we're always going to be cranky when he takes us out. He's even said that he likes to see us unhappy when he takes us out. But he's the manager, so he's looking at the big picture, too. He wants all of the starters to make it through the end of the season and, hopefully, the postseason. Garza just pushes his buttons a little too much with what he says. As with most conflicts on this team, thee two of them will quickly work out their differences and move on.

One thing we've been doing this season is beating the teams we're supposed to beat. Good teams do that. Garza's win over the Orioles gives us a 10–3 record against them this season. The idea is to beat the teams you're supposed to beat and slug it out to .500 or a little better against the heavyweights. A couple of other cool things happen in this game. The win gives us our fortieth road win of the season, matching our total for 2008, when we won the division and went to the World Series. Ironically, we crushed opposing teams at Tropicana Field that season—our home record was just sick—but somehow we've lost some of our good karma at home. Who can figure that stuff out? You would think that we'd always have a home field advantage as long as we play at Tropicana Field. There aren't any other ballparks like it in the major leagues. It's particularly tough on outfielders who have not played there before, because you can easily lose a fly ball against the background of the roof.

Something else I'm kind of proud of—because I had something to do with it, as did a lot of the guys in our clubhouse—is that the win against the Orioles gives us a 391–391 record under Joe. It's the first time he's had a .500 record since getting off to an 8–8 start in his first season managing the club.

Joe is the only manager I've known in the major leagues. He managed the team when I came up in 2006, and he's been the manager ever since. I didn't think much about him when I first came up. When I got called to the major leagues, the last thing I worried about was who was managing the team. My main concern was to do everything possible to stay in the major leagues, so I didn't notice how unique a manager Joe is. I had been around minor-league managers, all of whom were different, but they weren't as different as Joe.

Joe is a baseball lifer. Prior to taking over the Rays, he spent 31 years in the Angels' organization, signing with the Angels as a free agent catcher in 1975 and playing through the 1978 season before moving into scouting and managing. During his tenure with the Angels, he did just about everything from scouting, coaching, and managing at the minor-league level to filling the role of bench coach for Angels manager Mike Scioscia. Joe was a part of the 2002 Angels team that beat the San Francisco Giants in the World Series. Anybody would get a baseball education traveling the path he's traveled. Add to that the fact that he's a smart guy, he's positive, and he has incredible people skills, and you've got quite a manager.

The perception of him can be misleading because he wears those goofy Buddy Holly glasses, he likes to have fun, and he is so positive. He never airs out a player to the media or in public view, but he's not afraid of being firm behind closed doors. The longer I play for him, the more I realize how special he is and the more I appreciate him. I credit the organization's management for recognizing that Joe could be a special manager when they put forth their search to replace Lou Piniella as the team's manager after the 2005 season. Obviously, they looked beyond the fact that Joe never played in the major leagues—and that he looks at things a little differently.

Well, I'll be going for my fourteenth win tomorrow night. Hopefully I can keep us in the game and we can cut the Yankees' lead.

Standings on September 3

Tm	W	L	GB
NYY	85	50	--
TBR	83	51	1.5
BOS	76	58	8.5
TOR	69	65	15.5
BAL	49	86	36.0

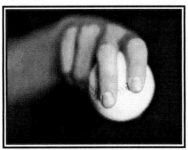

Four-seam fastball

FOUR
September 4-8

I'M AN EARLY-MORNING GUY, particularly on days when I'm pitching. I like to get up and get moving around. The morning of my start in Baltimore, I leave the hotel and walk some. I get a little breakfast and think about the Orioles, our season, and my pitching.

I don't think I'm having a bad season, but the numbers say otherwise. Entering tonight's game, I have a 13–11 record with a 4.73 ERA. That ERA feels inflated relative to my own assessment of my pitching. Unfortunately, a lot of being a successful pitcher at the major-league level is the ability to limit the damage. Take away a couple of the starts I've had this season, and my ERA would be a full point lower. But those are the breaks. I haven't done a good job of damage control on certain occasions, and that's what my numbers reflect.

As it turns out, my start against the Orioles isn't any different.

I made my first major league start at Camden Yards and have always considered it one of my favorite places to pitch. Like hitters,

41

pitchers favor certain parks in which the sight lines, the mound, or any number of little things just make them feel more comfortable. I feel good about performing in Camden Yards, and I feel confident heading into the start.

The temperature at the beginning of the game is 75 degrees, and the air is muggy under overcast skies. Not bad weather to pitch in. I like to pitch when it's warm. You sweat a lot and you have to worry about getting dehydrated, but it's easier to stay loose.

John Jaso gets us off to a good start with a home run off Jeremy Guthrie to start the game. Talk to any pitcher in the major leagues, and he'll tell you that walking to the mound with an early lead is one of the best things that can happen. I head for the mound in the bottom of the first telling myself to be aggressive with the early lead, but that plan doesn't work so well.

Brian Roberts leads off the Orioles' half of the first by lining my fourth pitch into left field for a single. Then I get behind 3–0 to the next hitter, Nick Markakis, and after fighting back to get the count to 3–2, he homers to right-center field.

Markakis's home run doesn't bother me. I've given up a bunch of home runs; it's an occupational hazard when you throw strikes like I do. What gets under my skin is giving up a two-spot. Most of the homers against me are solo shots. After that I settle down to retire the next six hitters, striking out two.

In the Baltimore half of the third, however, the night really starts to go downhill.

Cesar Izturis and Markakis both single and are on first and second with one out when I run into a little bad luck. Ty Wigginton grounds to Evan Longoria at third, and Longo fields the ball, but the play develops kind of funny. In the end, he has to throw to first because of the timing on the play, and Wigginton beats the throw to load the bases. So there's only one out instead of two when Luke Scott comes to the plate. The count goes to 3–2, and I throw him a good change-up that goes in the dirt. He appears to go for the pitch, but home-plate umpire Bill Welke rules that Scott checked his swing and calls the pitch ball four. (Later I watch the pitch again on video, and I'm still convinced Scott swung.) The walk drives in a run. Felix Pie then flies out to right field, driving home a run, to bring up Matt Wieters with two outs.

Situations like this are tough to deal with sometimes. You're out there on the mound, and you know you should be out of the inning. Instead two runs have scored and you still have two men on base. Getting frustrated never helps anything, though. All you can do is look at what's ahead of you, which means dealing with Wieters. Unfortunately, he gets me for a double down the right-field line to drive home two. That puts the Orioles up 5–1.

In the fifth I get Wigginton to fly out to right, then Scott follows with a double to center on my seventy-sixth pitch of the game. Normally I feel like I'm just getting loose after 76 pitches, but when I look over toward our dugout, I see Joe coming out to give me the hook. I can't believe it and I'm not too happy about it.

Meanwhile, Guthrie pitches a pretty good game. After giving up that one run in the first, he allows just one more in seven innings, and we lose 8–4. Guthrie gets the win, and I take the loss—the first in my last four games—to move to 13–12 on the season. My ERA moves up to 4.92, which is much too close to 5.00 for my comfort level. The worst part is that we fall back to 2½ games behind the Yankees. We haven't been that far behind the Yankees since August 8.

I get to the ballpark on Sunday still feeling a little steamed about getting taken out so early, which leads to a meeting with Joe. When I ask him why he yanked me, he explains that the game wasn't going our way, and he didn't want me to waste any more pitches. He wanted to save some bullets. It's the same explanation he gave Garza, and it sounds reasonable. I get it, but at the same time I'm still upset. I'm a competitor. I compete every day. I don't want to get taken out at 76 pitches. I'm a big team player, but I also have my own goals. I tell Joe, "I've been the workhorse since 2006 in this organization. I've been a guy who can go deep into a game no matter how many runs I give up. I'm able to go 100, 110 pitches."

Then Joe tells me that he had Jeremy Hellickson up in the bullpen, and knowing that Hellickson had already warmed up, he didn't want to disappoint him. He felt like he had to get Helly into the game. That gets me a little more pissed. I don't feel that I should be taken out to accommodate Hellickson—especially when we're in the middle of a pennant race. But Joe does what he has to do. He's that kind of manager. He definitely has his own way. You've got to respect that.

Right after my start I begin the work that nobody sees. Starting pitchers work pretty hard between starts. You put your body through a lot during the season, so you have to put in the work or your body is going to fail you. All the muscles in the body—particularly your legs—determine how healthy your arm is going to be. Maintaining your strength is a large part of the equation.

Unless I throw a whole lot of pitches during a game, like 110 to 120, I'll follow my start with an upper-body weight workout after the game. But the real work begins the day after my start, when I do a heavy workout with my legs. Each of the starting pitchers has his own leg routine. After I'm finished, I'll do a 20- to 25-minute cardio workout. Sometimes I'll go out and run three miles, or I might do some cardio inside.

The second day is my bullpen day. I throw every day—as do the other starters—but the bullpen day is the only day when I throw off a mound between starts. I'll usually throw 35 to 40 pitches during a normal bullpen.

Some days are shorter than others, depending on how well I'm doing. After I'm done throwing, I'll go back to the clubhouse and do some cardio, usually 20 minutes on a stationary bicycle.

I do another leg workout on the third day, but with lighter weights. Afterwards, I'll do some cardio work, either "poles"—running on the warning track from foul pole to foul pole–or sprints, depending on whether we're playing outside or inside.

Finally, on the day before I pitch, I like to go out onto the field and shag fly balls during batting practice—that gets my blood flowing. I also throw from 90 feet and run sprints. Once that final workout is complete, I'm ready for my next start.

In addition to the physical work, we pitchers do "classroom" work as well. We study videos of the team we're going to pitch against, and we go over scouting reports to get ideas about the tendencies of the hitters we'll be facing.

Wade Davis starts for us in the series finale against the Orioles on Sunday afternoon, so we feel like we have a pretty good chance. Last year he came up at the end of the season and pitched a complete-game shutout against the Orioles at Camden Yards. We really want to get the win so we can take the three-game series. All major-league teams think in terms of winning a series. Facing a 162–game season, you don't want to look at all of those games at once. Instead, you split up the season into chunks. Players are always looking to the next series. If you win one series after the next, you're going to have a pretty good record by the end of the season. Series wins are big.

Our bats come alive against Orioles starter Chris Tillman. B.J. Upton, Ben Zobrist, and Evan Longoria all homer. But the biggest story line of the game is that Rocco Baldelli comes off the bench to pinch hit in the seventh inning and responds with a two-run homer, giving us four for the game. Unfortunately, despite scoring runs, we lose the game 8–7.

Rocco joined the Rays' organization in 2000 after being selected in the first round of the draft. He advanced through the organization quickly and arrived in the major leagues in 2003 looking like he would be everything he was forecast to become when he was brought aboard, a true five-tool player who could hit for average and power, had a strong arm, and could field and run. On top of all of that, he brought a presence to the clubhouse. Everybody liked Rocco. Unfortunately, he started breaking down even before I got to the major leagues. Injuries and a mysterious health ailment finally brought an end to his time with the Rays. He suffered from excessive muscle fatigue that was diagnosed as a mitochondrial disorder, which forced him to constantly monitor what would zap him of his energy. He went through all kinds of tests just to get back on the field and ended up rejoining us late in the 2008 season and playing for us in the World Series. After that he signed with the Red Sox and had modest results during the 2009 season. He continued to have bad luck, though. An injury to his shoulder while playing for the Sox put his career on hold.

The Rays brought him back this past spring as a "special assistant," which called for him to work in a myriad of jobs within the organization. A lot of people speculated that he might be back in uniform at some point. After all, he had been a special player. And that's what happened. He began playing in minor league games in August, then joined the parent club.

I think everybody gets a lift when Rocco pinch hits. Matt Joyce usually doesn't get to hit against left-handers, and since Mike Gonzalez, a left-hander, is pitching, Joe sends Rocco to the plate. Amazingly, on the first swing of his first at-bat after rejoining the team, Rocco lofts that two-run homer into the left-field stands. Joe calls it a "great moment for us as a group," and I couldn't agree more.

Longoria's home run gives him 20 for the season. As if I didn't already know how special a player he is, I saw a note by the Elias Sports Bureau that said Longo—I like to call him "Lango"—is one of five players in modern baseball history to hit 20 or more homers and 30 or more doubles in each of his first three major-league seasons. The other guys who have done it are Joe DiMaggio, Albert Pujols, Orlando Cepeda, and Ted Williams. Not a bad group to be connected with.

Lango had "it" from the moment he came up with us early in 2008. Funny how one player has "it" and another doesn't. Carl Crawford easily is the best player in franchise history—he's got all the numbers, he's a great athlete, and all of that—but Lango became the face of the team almost immediately, because he has "it." He just became the guy. His name is catchy, of course, since Eva Longoria is a star of the TV show "Desperate Houswives." But it's more than that, obviously. C.C. is a true superstar, but he's one of those guys who would rather operate under the radar a little bit. I think the fact that Lango likes being a leader stands out. He does a lot of things for the community and for kids, and on top of that he came up and produced immediately. When you can come up to the big leagues and put up the kind of numbers he has—better numbers than Alex Rodriguez, even—you're going to become a star. When you are younger than everybody else it is pretty unusual to become a leader. Back in the day, I think you had to be a veteran of several years to become a leader. Normally, when you're a rookie, you're just trying to get your feet wet. But Lango did a great job of stepping up. We have a young team, which made stepping up a little easier, but he's become the leader of the team. He plays the game the right way.

When you become "the guy" and have "it," you also get to enjoy the trimmings that come with said designation, such as endorsements. In Lango's commercial for New Era caps, which came out this spring, somebody had supposedly stolen his hat. The whole spot was pretty clever, combining elements from James Bond and Ferris Bueller, but he sure got abused for it in the clubhouse. We took his hat and messed around with him mercilessly, but he takes everything well.

Leadership, to me, means leading by example. If you do a great job with your workouts, if you do a great job with the way you play the game, and if you play the game hard every single inning and every single out, you can go up to guys and explain how to do things because you know in your heart that you do things the right way. I think that's how you become a leader, because the other players watch you and pay attention to how you play. You run hard to first on a routine ground ball, and you leg out doubles when you have to. You play the game the right way. Then the other players start listening, too. That's where Longo is. He's at the point where he's helping out a lot of guys and trying to make everybody do things the right way. The bottom line is that he wants to win.

Losing two-out-of-three to the Orioles reminds me a little bit of the old days with the Devil Rays. Baltimore is out of the race, but they're dangerous. I remember what it felt like being way out of it long before the final month of the season. Either the Red Sox or the Yankees would be at the top of our division looking down on us in the cellar, and it was terrible. When you're that far out of it, you have to do something to stay in the game. Late in the season, we had to psyche ourselves up. Back in 2007, which was the last year we wore green uniforms and were called the Devil Rays, we began to play well in August.

Heading into August, we were 24 games out of first place with a record of 40–66. Baseball is a long season. You play 162 games. When you're as far out as we were, that 162–game season can feel like a prison sentence, except that it didn't really feel that way at the end of the 2007 season. We had a lot of talent on our team and we could play any one game like we were the best team in baseball. Comments would trickle out of the other clubhouses about how they did not like to play us because we had such a young and athletic team. We just didn't know how to win yet. We'd never won before, and we really didn't have any leaders on the team who could show us what it took to win at the major-league level. But everything seemed to come together that August, and we ran off a 15–14 record, giving us our only winning month of the season. We beat the Yankees once and even managed to beat the Red Sox a couple of times. We finished the season with an 11–16 September, giving us another last-place finish in the American League East with a 66–96 record, but we had played hard down the stretch. There's no telling how valuable finishing the 2007 season the way we did was for us the following season, when we finally broke through to win our division and go to the World Series. We had gained a lot of confidence.

That's the way the Orioles are this year. They're not just finishing out the season. They're building for next season. When we were in that situation, we didn't want the Yankees and Red Sox to go to the postseason, and we wanted to be the reason they didn't make it. Baltimore is like that now. They wanted to beat us, and that's what they did. They want to do the same thing against the Yankees and Red Sox. They want to be the spoilers. I talk to a few of their guys, Markakis, Scott, and Adam Jones. They all say, "Hey man, we're not going away." They're also playing for their career numbers and their season stats. Every player has to do that, since numbers define you and dictate how you are paid. That's the major leagues.

After playing our final game against the Orioles, we board a plane and fly to Boston to begin a three-game series with the Red Sox. The thing we're looking forward to most in this series is having the chance to knock them out of the race. They may not be mathematically eliminated if we take two out of three, but it will be damn hard for them to get back into the race. We'd have to lose ten straight games or so. Taking two out of three will pretty much ensure that we're going to make the playoffs either by winning the division or as the wild-card team.

Jeff Niemann starts the first game against Boston. I always like our chances when he's on the mound, because there aren't many pitchers like him. He stands 6-foot-9 and uses that height to make things tough on the hitter. Not only does Jeff have all the pitches, he delivers the ball at a steep downward angle. Batters aren't used to seeing the ball come at them from the top of the mountain. But he's still having a tough time since returning from the disabled lists, and Boston gets him for six earned runs in 1 $\frac{2}{3}$ innings.

At times the numbers of the game can be cruel. In the three games since he's been back from the disabled list, he's allowed 23 earned runs in 10 innings. When you're in that situation, you feel like you're letting everybody down. I know the feeling. In reality, everybody on the team knows what Jeff can do and that he's just having a hard time getting back into the groove. You just want to go out there and get some better results.

Crawford continues to destroy the Red Sox on the base paths. He steals his thirty-fifth consecutive base against them without being caught—they haven't managed to gun him down since September 21, 2005. Crawford's excellence aside, we take a 12–6 loss to remain 2 $\frac{1}{2}$ games behind the Yankees, who also lose.

David Price starts for us the next night, September 7. He's been locked in all season, and at Fenway Park he brings his "A" game again. Ironically, the one guy on our team who hasn't needed much run support lately receives a boatload. Our guys are really hitting. Ben Zobrist, Jason Bartlett, Evan Longoria, Dan Johnson, and B.J. Upton all homer, establishing a single-game high for the season. We finish with 14 hits on the night, and a couple of the innings last so long that Price has to go back to the clubhouse to pedal a rickety stationary bike to stay loose.

We needed Price to come up big, too, since our starters—me included—have allowed 16 earned runs in 11 innings in our last three losses. A true No. 1 starter is supposed to go out and stop a tailspin, and that's what our team looks for Price to do when he goes out there. That's another reason why he'll probably be the No. 1 starter for us next season. He's driven, and he's got incredible skills. Most guys would like to have just one of those qualities. He has both, which makes for an amazing combination.

Price holds the Red Sox to one earned run and two hits in six innings to pick up his seventeenth win of the season. Hellickson takes over for him in the seventh and experiences a little bit of a rough stretch that sees the Red Sox score three in the 1 $\frac{2}{3}$ innings he pitches. Dan Wheeler and Mike Ekstrom finish off our 14–5 win. Crawford continues to make his case for becoming the highest-paid free agent in the coming off-season, going four-for-four with two RBIs. He leads the major leagues with eight four-hit games this season. Included in today's performance are three doubles in his first three at-bats against Daisuke Matsuzaka, who starts for the Red Sox.

C.C. has amazing talent. He's easily been the most consistent guy on the team offensively. He can do so many things, but most importantly, he reaches base a lot, and once he's on he knows how to get into scoring position. A walk or base hit is as good as a double for him, because he'll steal second like he owns the base. In recent years I've seen and heard certain statistical experts who diminish the value of a stolen base. What those guys don't understand, or can't quantify, is what a guy like C.C. can do to the defense. An infield will basically go into panic mode the second he steps into the batter's box. Infielders rush their throws, knowing they've got to get the ball to first quickly to beat him to the base, and sometimes you'll see that mindset make them bobble the chance. And if C.C. reaches base, the hitters that follow him know they're going to see a steady diet of fastballs, since the pitcher becomes afraid of throwing his breaking stuff for fear of C.C. stealing second or third base. He's a run-scoring machine. Add to that the fact that he seems to always come through in pressure situations, and you have a pretty special player.

Nobody really believes that C.C. will be back with the Rays next season, because a lot of teams are going to want him. I wouldn't be surprised if the Red Sox get into the bidding, based on the way he's played against them throughout his career. They might want to acquire him just so he doesn't beat them as often as he has in the past. But most people are speculating that he'll be playing for the Angels next season—grass outfield, great weather, nice payroll. We'll see. One thing's for sure, he leaves everything on the field every time he plays. What an incredible athlete. I think he could have been a professional athlete in any sport he chose. Sometimes on the scoreboard at Tropicana Field they'll show videos of C.C. when he played quarterback for Jefferson Davis High School in Houston, Texas. His team ran a veer offense. Different plays are shown, but all of them end up the same: C.C. reads the defense, keeps the ball, turns the corner around some dazed defensive end, and suddenly he's in the open field heading for the end zone. In one game he scored five touchdowns. He even scored a touchdown running back an on-side kick. His coach had put him on the field as part of the "good-hands" team, and when the ball bounced to him, he tore off to the end zone for about 50 yards.

He was offered a scholarship to play football for the University of Nebraska, which would have been interesting because he would have been there at the same time as Eric Crouch, who won the Heisman Trophy in 2001 while playing quarterback for the Cornhuskers. Crouch was an exciting player and could do a lot of things. Running the football was more his strong suit than passing—which is probably why he never made it in the NFL—but you have to wonder if Crouch would even have started for the Cornhuskers had Carl been there. That's a question that can never be answered, but I just can't see Crouch being a better athlete than Carl.

Sports Illustrated recently conducted a poll among major league players, and C.C. was voted by his peers as the fastest player in the major leagues. If he goes somewhere else, I'll sure miss him. He's been a great teammate, and he's a great player to have on your team.

Every time we head to Boston, I'm reminded of the 2008 season and the best punch I never landed. The series of events that resulted in that punch being thrown began during a game that took place on June 4, 2008 at Fenway Park. In the sixth inning of that game, Coco Crisp stole second base, making a head-first slide. Our shortstop Jason Bartlett saw the way Crisp was sliding, so he dropped his knee between Crisp and the bag. Apparently, Crisp jammed his thumb on the play and took exception to Bartlett's tactic. He decided to get even in the eighth after he walked. Once again Crisp attempted to steal second, but this time he went in with his spikes high toward our second baseman, Akinora Iwamura. Anyone looking at the play and seeing the slide would have thought Crisp was trying to break up a double play. Nobody in our dugout liked what happened. Everybody felt like something had to be done, but nothing could be done in that game since Crisp didn't hit again. Retribution fell to the next day's starter, yours truly.

I knew my start wasn't going to last long. First I hit Dustin Pedroia—the Red Sox second baseman (get it?)—with a 94–MPH fastball. J.D. Drew then singled off me, and Manny Ramirez hit a bomb to give them a 3–0 lead in the first. Then, when Crisp came to the plate in the second, I hit him in the left thigh.

I feel confident that he knew what was coming. He'd told Carlos Pena before the game that he knew he was going to get hit. Still, he made the decision to come out to the mound even though I hit him clean, right on the thigh. I hit him the right way. You don't want to head hunt, but you do want to serve notice to the other team. The message is, "If you try to hurt my players, there's going to be retaliation."

When Crisp charged toward me, I didn't know what to do. As he flipped off his helmet and continued toward me, my instincts took over and I threw a huge haymaker at his face with my right hand and missed. Imagine that: the best punch I've ever thrown, and I whiffed. Good thing I did, too, because there's no telling what that punch would have done.

Our catcher, Dioner Navarro, tackled Crisp from behind, then all hell broke loose on the field. Once they broke up the fight, I got ejected and so did Jonny Gomes, our designated hitter—and designated enforcer.

In the aftermath of that little scrum, five of our players got suspended for a total of 23 games. Edwin Jackson got five games, Carl Crawford got four, Iwamura got three, Gomes got five, and I got six.

A lot of us believed that incident did more to hurt the Red Sox than anything else that year. We rallied after that, and the whole thing seemed to bring our team closer together. Beating the hell out of the Red Sox became a priority for us the rest of that season, and we pretty much did. Before that game, we could never beat them at Fenway Park. After the brawl, we played them tough in Boston.

I still think about that fight a lot. For some reason, it's remained a constant topic of conversation at the family Christmas party every year. Growing up, I wasn't a fighter, so I always wondered if I would ever get in a big-league brawl and what would happen if I did. Well

I did, and I got my answer to what would happen when I couldn't land the punch.

I don't know if it's just me, or if the other guys on the team feel the same way, but I don't really think there's any remaining bad blood between the Red Sox and us. To be honest with you, I actually like a lot of the guys on that team. There are definitely moments in a game when you don't like them. They might do something you think is a little dirty. But off the field, every baseball player is pretty much the same, and we have respect for one another. Once the lights turn on, though, we don't like them.

Garza starts the final game of the series.

Garz is one of my best friends. We're both from California— "Cally Boys"—so that didn't hurt. We also knew a lot of the same people, so we hit it off from the start. I'm telling you, Garz is in his own world. Mostly he just cracks me up because he does stupid stuff. We make fun of him. Most anything that comes to his mind, he'll say. He doesn't hold anything back, so he makes everyone laugh. He acts just like a little kid sometimes. He'll sit there in his hoodie with his DVD player, laughing out loud at the same episode of the same show he's watched a thousand times. Garz and Jason Bartlett came to us in a trade with the Twins prior to the 2008 season. Both of those guys were major players in helping us win the division that season. Garz is a great guy, but I think some guys just don't get him. He's quirky no doubt, but he's got a big heart. And when he's pitching, he's got filthy stuff.

One thing most people don't know about Garz is that he majored in civil engineering at Fresno State. He wanted to get educated in a profession that could earn him a good living. School came first for him and baseball second, because he thought he was going to be a civil engineer, which is not an easy major. Minnesota ended up drafting him in the first round of the 2005 June draft, the twenty-fifth pick overall, so he reversed fields and made baseball his top priority. Based on what he's accomplished and the money he's made, Garz appears to have made the right decision. This year he threw the first no-hitter in Rays history when he no-hit the

Tigers back in August. Given his stuff, the biggest surprise to me is that he'd never thrown a no-hitter before that, though he had come close. He cares about winning a lot. The big misperception about him is that some mistake his quirkiness for being indifferent toward winning, which is totally wrong. He wants to win more than anybody.

Garz and his wife have three kids, and when he's playing with them you can't tell him from the kids. But he's a great dad. We've had them over to the house for barbecues, and he's always playing with his kids. He's the guy every kid wants as a dad—someone to lie around and watch cartoons with or play video games with, because that's what he enjoys doing. I won't deny that I enjoy watching cartoons myself. I'll just say I don't enjoy them quite as much as Garz does. Seemingly, he loves every show on TV. He loves "That 70's Show," "The Office," and "Two and a Half Men."

Garza's emotions and his quality stuff are perfectly suited for October baseball. Once you reach October, everything gets tuned up a couple of notches. He has what it takes to be involved in a game that's taken to the next level. To me, that makes him a quality commodity.

Garza has always done well against the Red Sox, so the team always seems to carry a little bit of a swagger when he starts against them. It's like we know we're going to beat them when he's pitching. Of course, over the years, our group of guys has gone from not knowing how to win, to expecting to win every night. That's a tough feeling to acquire. But on the nights Garza pitches against the Red Sox, the feeling that we're going to win is amped up even more, and that's particularly true given the way he's been pitching lately. He's gone 3–2 with a 1.32 ERA in his last six starts.

The visiting clubhouse at Fenway Park is close quarters, to say the least. With an expanded roster in September, you feel like you can't move in there. On the one hand it's kind of claustrophobic, but on the other it's kind of cool. Everybody's right there with everybody, so you see more of your teammates. There's a TV in the middle of the clubhouse with two ornate couches that everybody lounges on. A lot of times there will be a movie playing before the game, but when we arrive at the clubhouse on this afternoon, the TV is tuned to the Yankees-Orioles game.

We all arrive at the clubhouse understanding the significance of our game. If we win, we have another series win, and a big one at that. But we get some bad karma prior to the start of the game. While Garza munches his Popeye's chicken and watches his DVD, we all huddle around watching the Orioles play the Yankees. Baltimore's ahead going into the bottom of the ninth, and we're all feeling pretty good about the whole thing. Baltimore clipped us a little bit, and now they're taking care of business with the Yankees. Then Nick Swisher hits a two-run, walk-off homer at Yankee Stadium to give the Yankees a 3–2 win. Talk about a mood killer.

Ball players always say we don't pay attention to what other teams are doing; we just take care of our own business. Truth be known, though, we do pay attention to what the other teams are doing. When Swisher goes yard, most of us feel like we've been hit in the stomach. Like no matter what, the Yankees are going to find a way to win. That changes the vibe in the clubhouse a little bit. Instead of going out there hoping that we'll win and the Yankees will lose, we go out there hoping to win and not lose ground against the Yankees. It's just a different feeling.

Once on the field, the Red Sox take it to us.

Fenway Park is packed as usual. There's a different feeling among their fans this year. Normally they expect their team to win. It's almost like arrogance. But with all the injuries this season, they kind of view their team as an underdog, and as anybody who watches sports knows, pulling for the underdog is always the best kind of allegiance. The feeling I get among Red Sox fans is that anything the team manages to salvage this season will be a bonus. If they come from behind to get a playoff spot, the season will truly be one to celebrate.

Early in the game our offense appears ready to pick up where it left off last night. Upton hits a three-run homer off Boston starter Tim Wakefield in the second inning. In the past, Wakefield has killed us with his knuckleball, but lately our guys have been having pretty good success against him.

Like C.C., B.J. is a thorn in Boston's side. Of his 16 homers thus far this year, five of them have come against the Red Sox. He's hitting .350 in his last six games, which could bode well for us given the way B.J. has hit in the past. In the 2008 postseason, he helped carry the offense when he hit seven home runs in 16 games to tie an American League record for a single postseason. Four of those seven came in the American League Championship Series against the Red Sox. By the end of the postseason, B.J. came up one home run shy of Barry Bonds's record of eight home runs for a single postseason, which Bonds set in 2002. B.J. had left-shoulder surgery following the 2008 season and struggled some offensively. He never used the surgery as an alibi, but I don't think he was healed for a while—longer, at least, than he told everyone. If he gets going, he has the kind of bat that can carry a team.

Our offense builds up a four-run lead, which normally would be plenty of runs with Garz on the mound, but the Red Sox begin to chip away at the lead in the second when Adrian Beltre hits a two-run homer. Then Marco Scutaro and David Ortiz add solo home runs in the third to tie the score. Bartlett gets the lead back in the fourth with an RBI double, but we just can't seem to put them away. Victor Martinez ties the score at 5–5 when he homers to lead off the fifth.

Garz continues to go after them with fastballs, and he looks like he has good stuff, but they continue to hit him. After the game, Garz will make the comment that the way they were spinning on him when he threw his breaking stuff, it was almost like they knew what was coming before he threw it. You never want to think that kind of spying is taken place, but you'd be naïve not to think it could happen. There have been times at certain parks when I've wondered whether signs were being stolen, as supposedly happened on Bobby Thomson's famous home run in 1951.

Author Joshua Prager's 2006 book *The Echoing Green: The Untold Story of Bobby Thomson, Ralph Branca and the Shot Heard Round the World* alleges that the most famous home run in major league history happened in part because the Giants were stealing signals. According to Prager's account, Giants coach Herman Franks manned a post inside the home clubhouse, which sat in center field at the Polo Grounds. Watching with a telescope, Franks stole the signal from the opposing catcher, then relayed the pitch to his bullpen catcher, who signaled the Giants hitters. Branca, of course, surrendered the game-winning home run to Thomson, who became a national hero. I'm not saying that still happens, but sometimes as a pitcher you do get paranoid when hitters don't seem fooled by anything you're throwing. But that's one of those things a pitcher just has to live with. Whatever the case, Joe goes out to get Garz with one out in the fifth.

The Red Sox continue to rake our bullpen, scoring five more runs, and in the end we take a five-run loss to fall 2 ½ games behind the Yankees. Even worse, the Red Sox creep to within 6½ games in the American League Wild Card race.

We can't discount the Red Sox. They just won't go away. I think we need to embrace what Joe has been saying all along: "Until math says they're eliminated, they are not."

Even while we're getting our butts handed to us in Boston, I'm feeling anxious about my next start in Toronto.

On August 7, I started against the Blue Jays in Toronto, and the outcome wasn't pretty. Going into that start, I felt like I had it all together. I'd just pitched one of my best games of the season, getting the win against the Yankees at Tropicana Field after allowing one run in 7 ⅓ innings. I walked only one while striking out 11 in that start, but every start is different, which is something you learn in the major leagues.

I've had starts when I thought I had great stuff while warming up in the bullpen before the game, but then got lit up. And I've had starts when I felt like I had nothing, yet the next thing I know it's the eighth inning and I'm still in the game. You just never know what you're going to take to the mound from one start to the next.

So I went to Toronto for that August 7 start thinking I'd righted my ship with the good performance against the Yankees. Boy was I ever wrong. My performance against the Blue Jays was disgusting. Nothing went right for me that day. My rhythm was out of whack, my timing was bad, and I continually missed my spots. There's quite a group of hitters over there in Toronto, and they more than took advantage of my state. There are times when you're out there on the mound with nothing and you feel exposed, like a wounded animal in the wilderness. Sooner or later, you know you're going to get eaten alive.

J.P. Arencibia, a hot-shot catching prospect for the Blue Jays, started me down a bad road. I'd read the scouting reports on him and knew he could be a dangerous hitter. He did some nice things playing at Triple-A—32 home runs and 85 RBIs in 104 games—but when I saw that those numbers came while playing for Las Vegas, I wondered if some of his home runs were products of the thin mountain air out there. I love to play golf, and believe me, when you hit a golf ball out there it seems to go forever. I can hit a golf ball a long way, but never as far as when I'm playing in Las Vegas. A baseball, too, just goes farther in thin air. So anytime you see big numbers from someone playing in Vegas, you've got to temper those results with the knowledge of the climate where they were accumulated. Having said all of that, I believe Arencibia is legit.

He began a home run onslaught against me that afternoon when he homered to left in his first major league at-bat. Unfortunately, his home run wasn't the last the Blue Jays would hit that day. All told, they got me for six home runs. My line for the day was about as ugly as any I've had: eight runs on nine hits—including six home runs—in four innings. Add four walks to that, and that's about as bad as I can pitch.

All nine of their hits against me went for extra bases. My performance tied a major league record. I became the eighth pitcher in the Modern Era to serve up six home runs in a single game, and the first non-knuckleballing pitcher to do so since 1940. Prior to that game, my career-high for home runs allowed in a single game had been three.

After I left the game, the ball continued to fly out of the park. I don't know if the results had anything to do with the roof being open at Rogers Centre, but it felt a little bit like Vegas.

Arencibia added another home run after I left the game, and he finished with four hits in five at-bats. Not bad for a major-league debut. We ended up losing 17–11, and at the end of the day, Toronto set a new franchise record with eight home runs in a single game.

Thus, you can understand me having a little bit of anxiety facing the prospect of pitching in Toronto again. Like I've always said, though, if you're a pitcher, you have to have a short memory. Sometimes you get your butt kicked, and sometimes you don't. You just have to move on. I think one of the most important things in baseball is to have amnesia. You have to forget about things, just let them go. Otherwise those negative thoughts linger. You can't think about what happened in your last start or in any past start—you have to keep your focus on the one ahead.

The good news is that we're in a pennant race right now. I know I have to find a way to shut down Toronto. I think if we were dead last in the league it might be a little harder to forget about that outing against them. Toronto has a good team, but I'm going to go out there and trust my stuff. I know mechanically I'm pitching really well right now, save for a couple of little things I'm tinkering with. I've just had some bad luck.

Standings on September 8

Tm	W	L	GB
NYY	87	53	--
TBR	84	55	2.5
BOS	78	62	9.0
TOR	72	67	14.5
BAL	53	87	34.0

Changeup

FIVE
September 9-12

A QUALITY CHANGEUP IS A BASIC NECESSITY for any major league pitcher.

Most organizations won't even let a player go to the majors unless he has one in his pitching arsenal. The benefits of a changeup are immense, but it's a hard pitch to come by.

Obviously, the basic idea for the pitch is to make the hitter think he's looking at a fastball, only the ball arrives a lot slower. You achieve that effect by gripping the ball differently than you do a fastball, and therein lies the problem for most pitchers when trying to learn the pitch. Every pitcher has different-sized hands and fingers along with different arm slots and pitching strokes, which adds to the mystery of what will work for you. Finding the right grip is like a courtship. You date a few, but you're not really smitten. When you finally do find the right grip, you're in love, and you know you've found your mate.

My changeup is my best pitch, and I found it more out of necessity than anything else.

During one of my off-seasons when I was still in the minor leagues, I was playing catch with my brother Jeremy one afternoon in a lot across the street from my family's home in Valencia, California. I called Jeremy a pooh-slinger because he had been a crafty left-hander and only threw about 85 or 86 MPH. This was right after I had shoulder surgery. I was kind of bummed about my velocity, which had dropped below 90 miles per hour. You don't see a lot of right-handed pitchers in the major leagues who throw below 90 MPH, but if you're left-handed, that's another story. As famous broadcaster Skip Caray once said of Frank Tanana when the veteran left-hander was still pitching at an advanced age: "Here's Frank Tanana. If he wasn't left-handed, they'd be calling him coach." Left-handers have that luxury, while right-handers don't last long if they can't break 90 MPH with their fastball. At that time my fastball arrived at about 86 or 87 MPH—I was right there with Jeremy. Everybody told me that once the shoulder healed I'd regain my velocity, but I found that hard to believe, even though I desperately wanted to believe it. So I was dealing with that mentality while playing catch with Jeremy, who had a pretty nice changeup.

Since I didn't have my fastball back but wasn't ready to quit baseball, I knew I had to come up with something to get hitters out, and refining the changeup seemed like one of my best options. After experimenting with several grips, I found the one I still use today—love at first sight. I think my grip is unique, because I use certain elements of the circle change—which is the most popular changeup grip—but with some variations. Having been around the league for a while, I haven't found anybody else who grips the ball for a changeup the way I do. Most guys throw it using their middle finger, but I throw it off my index finger—my power finger—which allows me to stay behind the ball a little bit extra. Doing it that way gives the ball a little more depth. I consider the pitch to be a power changeup.

If a pitcher has a quality changeup he can throw for strikes and can locate his fastball, he's going to do well. A lot of guys in the majors don't have good breaking pitches and get by with a fastball-changeup combo, but the changeup is a tough pitch to come by.

Like I said, finding the right changeup required experimenting with a bunch of different grips before I fell in love, and I fell in love because of the out-of-kilter swings the pitch produces. You can split the middle of the plate with a changeup and still get that awkward swing. In my case, the hitter knows my fastball comes in around 92 or 93 miles per hour. My change is around 82 or 83. The idea is to make the pitch resemble a fastball coming out of your hand. If you're the hitter, you're seeing the ball coming toward you out of the same tunnel as the fastball, and you just can't judge the speed. The timing of a pitch is the difference between a soft-hit and a hard-hit ball, which is why the pitch is a great equalizer for a pitcher.

Even if you don't throw the changeup, hitters know if you have a good one, so they're always thinking that might be the next pitch they swing at, mistaking it for a fastball. Hitters don't like to look bad, and being on guard against a changeup can really mess with a hitter's timing. A lot of times that can force a hitter to be less aggressive.

A pitcher has to be careful, though. Hitters study our tendencies just as we study theirs, and if you're throwing a changeup too often, they will spit on your fastball and wait for the change. And when a major-league hitter gets what he's looking for, it's all aboard for a ride to the moon.

Again, my fastball was down during the years I was coming back from shoulder surgery, so I was throwing my changeup about 65 percent of the time. I didn't have the fastball I needed to really offset the pitch, so I began using my cutter more often. Simply showing your change isn't enough, though. You have to have command of it or hitters will just lay off the pitch and take it for a ball. Arm speed is important. You are striving to show the same arm speed you show when you are throwing your fastball. And you want to have movement. Side-to-side movement isn't good. Making the ball take a downward angle is much preferred, either down and to the right or just straight down.

I throw two different changes. One of them comes in a little straighter and has a little bit of depth on it. I'll usually use that one when I want to get a strike early in the count. My other changeup is different from my "get-me-over" change. It's more of a "putout change" and has an action resembling a splitter with a lot more depth. Either one of those changes can be tough to hit, even if the hitter is looking for it, because I can command it well.

My fastball had returned by the time I went to the major leagues for the first time on May 27, 2006, after left-hander Casey Fossum went on the disabled list for the Devil Rays. And I got off to a nice beginning. After getting a no-decision in my first start at Camden Yards against the Orioles, I won my next four starts. At that point I was thinking, "This is pretty easy." But major-league hitters make adjustments. Plenty of information is generated by advance scouts watching every major-league game, so pretty soon the word got out about my changeup. I was relying on it too much, and eventually I had to adjust to what the hitters were doing. Mostly what I needed to do was to base everything on fastball command.

Fastball command is everything to a pitcher, even if you have a pet pitch like the changeup. Command isn't just about throwing strikes. Command is throwing pitches wherever you want to—and need to—within the strike zone. Having fastball command allows you to set up all of your other pitches.

I've gotten to the point where I like hitters to be looking for my changeup. In fact, I love it when a guy is up at the plate sitting on my change, because I know that somewhere in the back of his mind, the fact that he's sitting on a changeup makes him uneasy. He knows that waiting for the change will let me easily beat him with my fastball. If a hitter's looking for a pitch that's going to come in around 81 or 82 MPH, you can throw him a fastball and it's going to make you look like the second coming of Nolan Ryan. The hitter just doesn't have time to catch up to the pitch. Some days you're ahead of the hitters in the thinking game, other days you're behind. And there's always the chance that the hitter runs into one of your best pitches, even though you've executed the pitch and he wasn't looking for it. But the better pitchers and the better hitters seem to win the mental battles on a more consistent basis.

Returning to Toronto, scene of the home run bonanza I allowed a month ago, takes a little bit of courage. You don't want to admit any kind of concern about having a bad outing, but six home runs are dancing in my head as we head into this game. I just have to remind myself that since that outing I have pitched some really good games, which has allowed me to rebuild my confidence. I'm a competitor, and I'm not about to let those six home runs break me down.

The offense helps me out big time by scoring six runs in the first inning, tying the team record for the largest number of runs scored in the first. You always feel fortunate to be the beneficiary of that kind of run support. Unfortunately, we almost let the game get away. They tie the game with a three-spot in the seventh inning, which costs me the win. It kills you to have a lead like 6–0 and not be able to finish off the deal to get the win. Getting a W is big no matter when you get it. I can't complain about the bullpen, though. I contributed to the nail-biter by allowing four earned runs in five innings.

A lot of what's going on for me right now comes down to not being able to locate my fastball consistently. Lately my fastball is just a little off the mark, and hitters have been crushing it. I've noticed, too, that I haven't been throwing my changeup for strikes, and when I'm not doing that, I create a lot of problems for myself. I've looked at a lot of video trying to figure out the answers, something I don't normally do because I want to avoid overanalyzing things. Most of my video work deals with identifying pitch locations and selections, how hitters are reacting to my stuff, that kind of thing. Then I try to make adjustments according to what I see. As a rule I don't look at mechanics, but I've felt a necessity to do so this year, and I've noticed a flaw.

I've been flying out of my delivery on occasion. When you're making the right delivery, you feel like you're throwing downhill and the ball just pops out of your hand, free and easy, out in front of your body. On a lot of the home runs I've surrendered this year, my left foot, or plant foot, has not come straight and flat when I've made my move to the plate. Instead, I've allowed myself to come down on the outside of my left foot, and that one little flaw throws the top of my body out of kilter. My left shoulder follows the foot to the outside, which in turn causes me to deliver the fastball high, and good things rarely happen when you throw high fastballs in the major leagues.

The problem is that a pitching motion is a lot like a golf swing. You can know what you're doing wrong, but it's hard to think about correcting the problem when you're on the tee box or the mound. You don't want to be thinking about mechanical stuff when you take the mound. In golf, you might realize that you're taking back the club from the outside through the inside on your follow through, which is causing a wicked slice, but you don't want to take that thought to the tee box with you. You want to have maybe one swing thought. Same thing goes for pitching. You don't want to take the mound worrying about a punch list of checkpoints in your delivery. You want one swing thought, not twenty, because if there are twenty things going through your mind, you're not going to throw well. You've got enough stuff to worry about while playing the cat-and-mouse game with the hitter. Once you take the mound, you want all of your mechanical issues ironed out so you can clear your mind and focus on the things you need to focus on. You don't want to think about how you're making your delivery. That's why you try to solve your mechanical issues between starts, just like a golfer heading to the driving range. As all golfers know, though, accomplishing that is a difficult task.

Fortunately for us, even though we blow the lead after I leave the game, we score a run in the ninth on a throwing error by their shortstop, Yunel Escobar. Rafael Soriano then shuts them down in the bottom of the ninth, getting the final three outs on strikeouts to preserve the win and earn his forty-second save of the season.

Soriano has been filthy all season, particularly the night he got his thirty-eighth save against the Angels. We were leading 4–3 in the ninth, and he used exactly nine pitches to strike out the side, becoming just the forty-fourth pitcher in baseball history to achieve that feat and the first to do so since Ross Ohlendorf did it for the Pirates in 2009. He struck out Erick Aybar on a foul tip, and Mike Napoli and Peter Bourjos then went down swinging to end the inning and the game.

Soriano can be pretty entertaining. After he completes a save, he pulls his jersey out from his pants. According to Sori, he's done with the job, so he's taking off his clothes. Most of us now do the same thing once he's chalked up another save. I call it "Shirts out for Soriano."

At the end of the day, I go from six home runs to two home runs against the Blue Jays. While that shows improvement, I'm never happy when I give up two home runs.

Wade Davis takes care of business on Saturday at Rogers Centre, holding the Blue Jays to one run on seven hits in seven innings of our 13–1 win to pick up his twelfth win of the season. That win gives him seven straight dating back to June 27, and by winning we move to within a half a game of the Yankees, who lose to the

Rangers 7–6 in Arlington.

Prior to the final game of the Toronto series, I get called into the manager's office. With a lot of managers, such a meeting can be quite an ordeal. With Joe Maddon, however, such meetings are never weird. He makes it easy because he has an open door. He's not one of those managers you have a difficult time talking to about stuff. He's open-minded. You can talk to him about whatever. Basically he tells me he wants me to reel in my emotions a little bit. A lot of times out there, I wear my emotions on my sleeve. I can't help it. I'm a competitor, and I get pissed when I mess up. There have been times when I've shown too much emotion when one of my teammates messed up behind me in the field, too. You never want to show up one of your teammates, so I've been wrong when I've done that. I can just imagine how I'd feel if somebody hit a bomb off me and one of the outfielders threw down his glove when the ball passed over his head and into the stands. Anyway, Joe feels like I've been getting out of my element, that I'm pressing too hard, and I agree with him. I need to get back to staying within myself and being competitive on the mound.

We finish our season series with the Blue Jays in disappointing fashion on Sunday. Jeff Niemann starts and allows three runs in five innings. We score two in the sixth to tie the game at 3–3 and add a run in the top of the ninth on a sacrifice fly by B.J. Upton to take a 4–3 lead, and that looks like money in the bank with Soriano coming in to pitch the ninth. But nobody's perfect. Even a guy like Soriano can give it up every now and then, and that's what he does. Adam Lind touches him for a two-run walk-off homer to give the Blue Jays a 5–4 win. Nobody can get upset with Soriano, since he's converted 19 straight save opportunities before this one. That's just going to happen from time to time.

If we could have pulled this one off we would be in first place, since the Yankees lose again in Texas by a score of 4–1. That win gives the Rangers a three-game weekend sweep and introduces some interesting dialogue about teams trying to manipulate who they will play in the playoffs.

Cliff Lee gets the win against the Yankees after holding them to two hits and one run through eight innings. Lee is about as good as they come in the major leagues—a tough left-hander who has good stuff and always seems to be a step ahead of the hitters. Texas traded for him back in July and suddenly they became a different team. Lately everybody has been talking about teams not wanting to face the Rangers in the first round of the playoffs for fear of having to face Lee twice in the best three-out-of-five division series. If you face the Rangers in a three-of-five series, you may well have to come up with a way to win all three games that Lee doesn't start, since he is likely to dominate his two starts like he has all season.

We didn't sweep the weekend series in Toronto, but we did claim our fourteenth road series of the season. That's huge, particularly since we've known all weekend that after finishing with Toronto we would return home to play the Yankees in a pivotal three-game series at Tropicana Field. We all knew the importance of staying in the moment for each game against Toronto, because the one cliché that is so true for any baseball player is that you have to take it one day at a time. But that's hard to do when the Yankees are waiting. I'm thinking to myself, "Here we are going toe-to-toe with the Yankees in mid September. Life in the major leagues doesn't get much more exciting than this."

I'm also looking forward to getting home to see my family. I've had an eventful year, beginning with my wife and me having our second child, another daughter. She was born in April, shortly after opening day, so she's almost five months old now. She's sleeping well. Everything is good. She's healthy and happy as can be, and she already has two teeth showing, which is really early. She's probably the happiest baby I've ever seen. My wife didn't want to have any more kids, but this one might change her mind. Now I think we might have a third. We're a truly blessed family.

Standings on September 12

Tm	W	L	GB
NYY	87	56	--
TBR	86	56	0.5
BOS	79	64	8.0
TOR	73	70	14.0
BAL	55	88	32.0

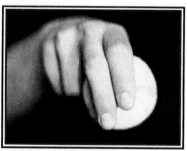

Cut fastball

SIX
September 13–15

GIVEN THAT WE'VE ONLY WON ONE DIVISION TITLE, there have been a lot of comparisons between this year's team and the 2008 team. Is this year's team better than the 2008 team? A lot of people have asked me that question, so here's what I think about that:

One big difference is that this year's team entered the season expecting to win. We know how to win, and a lot of the guys on the team were on the team in 2008 when the whole season played out like a fairy tale. Even at the end, when we finally lost to the Phillies in the World Series, we had that feeling that we were somehow going to figure out a way to win. We'd done so all season, so why wouldn't we find a way in the World Series? Unfortunately, the Phillies closed us out four games to one.

I think this year's team has played—and performed—with more pressure on us. Some experts might have seen what was coming in 2008, but they were a definite minority. We were pretty well off the radar screen as any kind of threat to win the division over the Yankees and Red Sox. I think we blindsided people in 2008. All season long, the other teams in the division, the media, and even the fans were just waiting for us to wake up one morning, realize we were in first place, and fall flat on our faces. We never did.

This season the other teams have come out to play us knowing that they'd better show up, because we can play. In that sense, I think we are a stronger bunch now because we had expectations going into the season and, for the most part, we've lived up to them. We haven't won the division or made the playoffs yet, though.

The 2008 season remains one of my greatest baseball memories. Winning is fun. Which leads me to what I believe is a misconception about this season not being as much fun as 2008. My point is, we're winning and that's fun. Again, winning is fun! The biggest difference this season is that we all know there's a good chance a lot of us won't be back with the team next year. That has placed a bittersweet element squarely behind all the joy of winning. We're such a close team, so it's sad to think we won't be back together. But we're professionals, and that's part of the game. All we can do is make the most of the remaining time we have together.

In 2008, our starting staff included Matt Garza, Scott Kazmir, Andy Sonnanstine, Edwin Jackson, and me. This year it's been David Price, Garza, Wade Davis, Jeff Niemann, and me. I think the 2008 staff was strong, but I think the big difference is Price. He's pitched like a true No. 1 starter all season. He might even win 20 games. So for starting pitchers I would give the nod to the 2010 team.

Our 2008 bullpen was strong with Troy Percival closing, and we had J.P. Howell, Trever Miller, Dan Wheeler, Jason Hammel, and Grant Balfour. Percival really brought a nice presence to our team and our bullpen. He had played on winners and knew how to win. I think his contribution to our success that season was huge. Percy got injured, though, which left us without a true closer. You are definitely stronger when you have a closer for the whole season. Rafael Soriano has been with us in that role all season. J.P. had left-shoulder surgery, so he hasn't been with us all season. That's hurt a lot, but Joaquin Benoit has been the eighth-inning guy and has been almost untouchable. Balfour, Wheeler, Randy Choate, Chad

Qualls, Lance Cormier, and Sonnanstine have been in the bullpen this season, too. So for bullpen strength I have to go with 2010 again.

On defense, we're just about the same team. Carl Crawford and B.J. Upton can run down anything in the outfield. We sometimes tease that those two are so fast and athletic that they could play a "cover-two" defense out there. Reid Brignac and Sean Rodriguez have been nice additions to the infield this season, but I have to say the defense between the two teams was too close to say one was better than the other.

I'd definitely have to give the nod for bench strength to the 2008 team, and I'm basing that entirely on the presence of Eric Hinske and Cliff Floyd that year. Both of those guys had been around, and they could still play. They also brought a boatload of intangibles to the team. Again, we were really wet behind the ears in 2008, but Hinske and Floyd gave us a sage, veteran presence in the clubhouse. Everybody looked up to those two guys, and they never disappointed.

Offensively it's probably a wash between the two teams. C.C. is having a better year this season than he did in 2008, but Carlos Pena had a better season in 2008.

Tabulating all the results, I'd have to say that this year's team is half a tick better than the 2008 bunch. But again, that team went to the World Series, and we haven't won anything yet this season.

In 2008, we basically had to beat the Red Sox, whereas this season the Yankees are our biggest obstacle to winning the American League East. That's why everything feels a little bit more alive when I go to the ballpark prior to Monday night's game against the Yankees. A lot of people in our clubhouse feel the way I do, and so do the Rays and Yankees fans and baseball fans in general. Baseball pennant races do that to anybody who loves the game. You play so many games, yet you're so close at the end, slugging it out when everybody's tired, as if you're in the late rounds of a classic heavyweight boxing match. I don't believe any sport can rival what happens in baseball in the fall.

And the pennant race isn't the only element of Monday night's game to get excited about. When I'm not pitching, I become a huge fan, and the pitching matchup between Price and CC Sabathia is so highly anticipated that Carl Crawford tells the media, "I'd pay to see that one."

Both of those guys are having great seasons, and in my opinion, they're battling it out for the Cy Young, though you can't forget about Seattle's Felix Hernandez, either.

Heading into the contest, Price has a 17–6 record with a 2.87 ERA. He has struck out 163 against 71 walks and has a 1.23 WHIP (walks + hits per inning pitched). He's won his last two starts. Sabathia brings a 19–6 mark and a 3.14 ERA into the game with 170 strikeouts, 66 walks, and a 1.21 WHIP. Baltimore hung a loss on Sabathia his last time out, which snapped a string of six starts in which he picked up the win.

Of course, there are differences between the two lefties. Sabathia came into the league at the age of 20 armed with a great fastball. He could just blow guys away. While he can still do that— his fastball registers in the 95 to 96 MPH range—he's become more of a command guy now. He'll repeatedly hit the same spot with his two-seam fastball, and he also has command of a four-seamer, a curve, and a changeup. So he's evolved from a hard-throwing lefty into more of a pitcher, which has a lot to do with why he has 155 career wins heading into tonight's game.

Whenever Sabathia pitches, you can bet Joe Girardi is thinking things like "complete game" and "rested bullpen." You can also rest assured that the Yankees manager is counting on a win from the big southpaw. That's because he's a true No. 1 starter—he's got the physical tools, and he knows how to pitch. He consistently carves up the lineups he faces. I think one of the more amazing things about Sabathia is that he just seems to get better and stronger as the season progresses. That's a real pro.

Price, on the other hand, is already great, but he hasn't reached the level he will. He'll tell you himself that he needs better command of his fastball so that he can throw the pitch whenever and wherever he wants. His changeup isn't there yet either, but his curveball is. The story of how he developed his curveball is amazing. He simply decided he wanted to throw one, and he worked on the pitch until he had refined it into what might be his best pitch.

There aren't a lot of pitchers in the major leagues that have really good curveballs, because it's a hard pitch to master. Most pitchers get frustrated trying to learn the curve and settle for a slider instead. There's more break to a curveball than a slider, and less velocity, which leaves more room for error. It's hard to throw a curveball for a strike because the pitch breaks so much. A slider is a compact pitch that's a lot easier to throw for strikes. You can attack the zone with it more easily. You throw it almost like a fast-ball, and it has a little bit of a slide to it. A curveball has a real big loop to it, and when you factor that in with the really tight strike zones that a lot of umpires maintain, it's understandable why throwing a curve for a strikes is so difficult. Price is one of the few major-league pitchers armed with a really strong curveball. Again, as good as he is, he's not nearly as good as he's going to be, given the way he works and the way he wants to be the best. That's got to be pretty scary if you're a hitter.

Everybody gets wrapped up in a pitching contest between two great pitchers—everyone, that is, except the pitchers themselves, if you believe what they're saying. They will tell you that the oppos-ing pitcher has no relevance whatever to what they are trying to do, and they're just going to concentrate on their own game. This is particularly true in the American League because pitchers don't even hit against each other. Still, say what you will, you know who you're pitching against, particularly when you are pitching against a big name. Price would never admit it, but he knows he's going up against Sabathia. And while it may be true that nothing Sabathia does will affect Price, a lot of pride is at stake. If you don't have that pride, you probably shouldn't be out there.

More times than not, these much-hyped match-ups don't meet expectations. One or both pitchers are off their game, and the duel of the gunslingers fails to materialize. But that isn't the case in the Sabathia-Price match-up at Tropicana Field.

Derek Jeter pokes a single to right off Price to start the game, then Robinson Cano grounds into a double play. After that, Price proceeds to set down in order the next twelve hitters he faces before Jorge Posada draws a two-out walk in the fifth. Posada gets thrown out trying to steal second, and Price sets down the Yankees in order in the sixth, which means he has faced the minimum number of hitters through six innings.

Of course, Sabathia matches Price zero for zero.

Both pitchers leave after eight innings. Sabathia has allowed just two hits and two walks while striking out nine, while Price has allowed three hits and two walks and has struck out four. Neither gets a decision, which means that Sabathia is denied his twentieth win while facing the Rays, and Price, for the second time in less than a year.

I don't care who you are or what team you're pulling for, watching those two match up is fun. In my book, anyone who has watched this game and doesn't think so can't call himself a real fan of the game. This is one of the best pitching performances from both sides that I've ever seen. Those two are the two most dominating left-handed pitchers in baseball, and watching from the bench is something special. Both of them are throwing 95, 96, 98 MPH. I'm telling you, those two guys are going to be legends. Future generations of baseball fans will talk about how hard they threw and how dominating they were in these games.

Things get a little bit dicey in the bottom of the ninth.

Kerry Wood takes over for the Yankees and strikes out Crawford looking. C.C. doesn't like the call and lets Tom Hallion know it, which prompts the home-plate umpire to run him. That kind of stuff seems to happen when you have a charged-up atmosphere like we have in this game. You hate to lose a player like C.C. at any time, but in this case it works out for us. Joe Maddon inserts Reid Brignac into C.C.'s spot in the order and puts him at second base, moving Sean Rodriguez to left field.

The flexibility of our team later allows Joe to pinch-hit Brad Hawpe for Jason Bartlett in the bottom of the tenth. Hawpe strikes out against Boone Logan to end the inning, then remains in the game in right field. Maddon then simply moves Ben Zobrist from right to second and Brignac from second to short.

Brignac doesn't get his first at-bat until he leads off the eleventh inning against Sergio Mitre—and what an at-bat. Brignac connects for his seventh homer of the season, a walk-off blast that gets Tropicana Field rocking. Suddenly we have a 1–0 win and a half game lead in the division. Brignac's homer was the only extra-base hit of the game and the first walk-off homer by a Rays rookie since Evan Longoria turned the trick on May 9, 2008, against the Angels. Winning that way is always exciting, but especially against the Yankees. They are a team we are always trying to beat year in and year out, so being able to do that to them in the opening game of the series charges us up a little bit extra.

What isn't special is the attendance. I can't believe Price vs. Sabathia isn't sold out. I don't understand the Tampa Bay fans. We go to other parks and play before sold-out crowds. Even the non-contending teams draw better than us. We've drawn just 26,907 tonight, and that's disappointing. You can never figure out if our home crowd is going to show or not. I remember the last home stand, when we drew over 90,000 for a three-game weekend series against the Red Sox and won two out of three games. Then the Blue Jays came to town and less than 40,000 showed up for the three-game series. Fans might not think so, but we really care about having fans in the stands. Having a good crowd gets us pumped up. There's just a different energy in this stadium when we have over 30,000 in the stands. We would love it if the fans would show up to see us play instead of deciding whether to show based on who we're playing. I know I've been on the team long enough to have played the Yankees and the Red Sox in games at the Trop that felt more like a Yankees or a Red Sox home game. I've heard about fans from both of those cities deciding that it's much easier to get tickets and cheaper for them to head to St. Petersburg to watch their teams play than staying at home to watch them play at Fenway Park or Yankee Stadium. I don't know what the answer is, but I can tell you that it's tough when you're playing for the Rays against the Yankees in your home park and all of a sudden you're getting your ears filled with "Let's Go Yankees!"

Garza starts the second game of the series for us and has a rough go of it, allowing six runs on nine hits in 4 2/3 innings. But we never give in, and in the fifth inning our offense breaks loose.

Pena opens with a home run against Ivan Nova. John Jaso, Lon-

September 13–15 / 75

goria, and Matt Joyce add RBI singles, then Willy Aybar finishes off the seven-run inning with a three-run homer to give us a 7–6 lead.

At that point, the Yankees have to be feeling the heat. After losing Monday night, the last thing they wanted to do was blow a 6–0 lead. But they quickly answer in the next inning, when Curtis Granderson doubles home a run to tie the game at 7–7, and that's how it stands through nine innings.

Posada pinch hits for the Yankees to lead off the tenth and comes through for his team, hitting a 2–0 pitch from Wheeler onto the top of the Batter's Eye restaurant in center field. Jeter follows with a single, prompting Joe to bring in Cormier. Wheeler gets heavily booed when he leaves the mound, and I feel bad for him. He's busted his butt for us ever since he's been here, and the booing is a shame. It's ironic—we normally have 10,000 fans for home games, and then for this one we get 20–25,000 fans, which is great—but they boo him. I think they're showing a lack of respect for what he's done— he's had a sub 3.00 ERA and has done a phenomenal job all season. It gets under my skin. I've been booed myself numerous times this year, so I know what it feels like. You want the fans on your side. You want them to cheer for you. It gives you extra motivation. But booing comes with the territory of being a baseball player. Even if you've been getting booed or you're getting booed at the time, you've got to get the job done.

None of the fans leave early. The game feels like a roller-coaster ride, with big ups and downs experienced by both teams. We have a chance to tie the game in the bottom of the tenth before a controversial play brings an end to the game.

The Yankees bring in No. 42 to pitch the tenth. That usually signals the end of the ballgame—Mariano Rivera and his filthy cutter are that good. But Crawford singles to lead off the inning, and after Longoria teases the crowd with a deep fly out to center field, C.C. steals his forty-third base of the season, bringing Joyce up to bat.

Whenever any of our guys faces Rivera, we just hope he can make contact so we'll at least have a chance to get something going. Joyce does just that, hitting a ball to right-fielder Greg Golson. Once Golson catches the ball, C.C. tags and takes off for third.

I don't think anything about C.C. tagging on the play. Nobody ever throws out C.C. at third. So what does Golson do? He delivers a strike to Alex Rodriguez, and the Yankees third baseman slaps a tag on C.C. for the third out. Game over; Yankees win 8–7.

The loss gives us an 87–57 record to the Yankees' 88–57 mark, flipping us in the standings and giving them a half game lead. The loss also brings out the second-guessers, who question how Crawford could allow himself to be thrown out going for third base with two outs.

One of baseball's oldest adages is not to make the first or third out at third. Since a runner on second is already in scoring position, the wisdom goes, he shouldn't try for third unless he's certain he can get there standing. The thing is, that rule just doesn't apply to C.C. He's one of the fastest players, if not the fastest player, in baseball, and you just don't expect him to get thrown out taking the free base that he normally owns. A storm of controversy starts right after the game. Everybody in the media wants to make a bigger deal out of what happened than it is or should be. They need to get it into perspective.

First, as Joe says right after the game, "Nobody died." Next, taking positive risks is one of the things we do on the Rays. Nobody read any positives into the possibility of Carl getting to third, so they surmised that his tagging and going on the play wasn't worth the risk, when in fact reaching third would have had great potential value. Remember that Rivera was on the mound, which means you have to do anything you can to advance, since there's no guarantee the next hitter is going to make contact. Even on the play itself, something good potentially could have happened. The throw from right field could have hit C.C. in the back, and the next thing you know he could have raced home with the tying run. He's got to take the chance on that. And again, you've got Mariano friggin' Rivera on the mound, the best closer in the history of the game. You've got to put pressure on him, which I think is what C.C. was trying to do. We were all telling him to go from the dugout. We're yelling "Go! Go!" We didn't know that kid in right field had a cannon for an arm. He's a rookie. But he threw an absolute seed to third, and he gunned down Carl.

To me, as a pitcher, a runner on third puts more pressure on you than a runner on second. Now, suddenly, if you have two strikes and you want to throw a ball in the dirt, you're taking a chance. If the catcher can't block the ball, the run scores from third on the wild pitch. I've also seen C.C. steal home, and every-one in the league knows he's capable of just about anything. Hav-ing him at third definitely would have put pressure on them, so he had to take the chance. Unfortunately, it didn't work out for us that time.

I love C.C.'s response to questions about the play the following day. He says, "I hope nobody gets too upset, because if that [situa-tion] comes up again, I'm going again."

Joe is the best at handling situations like that. He speaks to C.C. and tells him to take that base—always. I think you just have to chalk up that put-out to the rookie making a great play. I'm sure a lot of right fielders in the American League watched that play and couldn't believe what they were seeing.

Looking ahead, Joe and the powers that be decide to manipu-late the rotation so that Price can make one of the starts against the Yankees next week when we play them in New York. They don't like to fiddle with the rotation, but this is September and these are big games. Because we have an off-day on Thursday, Price can remain on regular rest yet still move up a day to pitch against the Angels on Saturday rather than Sunday. To accommodate the move, Jeff Niemann is moved back a day to start on Sunday.

Heading into my Wednesday night start against the Yankees in the series finale, I'm hoping to gain a little magic from my Afro, which continues to sprout. My hair is now 4 ½ inches long, and when George Hendrick, our outfield/first base coach, passes through the clubhouse before the game, I tell him that my hair reminds me of him back in the day. George fashioned a huge Afro during his playing days; now he shaves his head. He laughs at the observation.

George Hendrick, aka "Cuz," is one of the coolest guys around and great to have in the clubhouse. Not only was he a terrific ballplayer—18 major league seasons with six teams, a .278 career average, 267 home runs, and 1,111 RBIs—he's a voice of wisdom.

Cuz is amazing. He's 60 years old, but he's got the chiseled body of someone twenty years younger.

He's always got something going with everybody in the clubhouse, and he's got a great baseball mind. If you need the truth, you can go to Cuz and he'll give it to you. It might not be what you want to hear, but it's the truth. He is fun to be around, too. Cuz refuses to be quoted by the media, yet the media love him. I can't tell you how many times I've walked out to the dugout before a game, and he's there spinning old baseball stories in the animated fashion that is uniquely his.

Afro and Cuz aside, given the way I've been pitching this year and the way Garza kind of struggled in the second game, I have to go out there and be a bulldog and pitch my game. You tell yourself that going up against the Yankees is like pitching against any other team, but really it's not. It's definitely different. There's no doubt about it, particularly when you're fighting these guys for the division lead. You throw everything out that you've done during the season, and everything comes down to what happens in this game.

I don't plan to start the game with a set idea of how to pitch them. I want to take my cues from how they're swinging. I've already seen the scouting reports on the Yankee hitters, and I've tried to gain a fresh perspective and gather as much information as possible while watching Price and Garza go against them in the first two games.

A big difference between pitching in the major leagues and the minor leagues is charting pitches. The night before you pitch in a minor-league game, you normally sit behind home plate in your street clothes and chart the pitches for that night's pitcher. It's hard to imagine anything more tedious. We're baseball players, so we don't like to pick up a pen and write on a piece of paper. Once you get to the major leagues, you don't have to chart pitches anymore. I think it's assumed that we've been around the game long enough to remember what we're seeing, and we can augment our game-time observations with videos and other visual aids.

I pay close attention during the games, and watching what Price and Garza did has given me a pretty good idea how the Yankees' lineup is swinging the bats. Baseball is all about adjustments, so you never know where a guy might be during any point of the season. Despite all the preparation for a game, I always go into it with the mindset that I'm not going to try to do too much. You want to pitch to your strengths. I'm going into this game with a good feeling, since I had a really good outing against New York in my last outing against them, holding them scoreless and striking out ten in 7 $\frac{1}{3}$ innings here at Tropicana Field.

Robinson Cano has been the one guy in the Yankees' lineup who has really hit me hard—he has repeatedly bit my backside. He's such a great player. I have thrown him a couple of the nastiest pitches I've ever thrown and he has just crushed me. But I held him hitless in that last game, which was probably a first for me. I threw cutters in on his hands when he was probably looking for change-ups. He's a great changeup hitter. Still, I believe I have one of the better changeups in the league, so I'm going to throw it anyway, because I'm stubborn that way. Last game I tried to break off some curveballs against him, and I struck him out once or twice. And I definitely tried to get in on his hands to keep him from getting extended on me.

I've had pretty good success against Alex Rodriguez, even though he's one of the better hitters in the league. I try to pitch him in, too, and I don't think he likes the ball on the inner half. ARod likes to get his hands out. My four-seamer is straight and can get me ahead in the count, whereas my two-seamer has some downward action and will come in on his hands. I use that pitch for effect, to back him up and get him off the plate, make him uncomfortable. A lot of hitters these days wear elbow guards and shin guards—all kinds of stuff—so they don't worry about the high and inside pitch like they used to in the old days. I try to go inside for effect, to get the hitter off the plate a little bit, then maybe break off a curveball or a changeup down in the dirt.

All the planning and thinking about what I want to do against the Yankees seems wasted when I find myself in the first inning with my pitch count rising. I'm thinking, "Uh oh, here we go again." I'm making all of my pitches and doing everything I can to get outs, yet still they just happen to find some holes.

Here's a good example of why baseball has been called "a game of inches." I'm on the mound with the bases loaded, and Lance Berkman is at bat. Cano has just singled home a run, and I look over to Ben Zobrist at second base and say, "Hey, I need you to move about five steps to your left." And he says, "Why?" I say, "Don't worry about it."

Swinging at the first pitch after our exchange, Berkman hits a ground ball right to Ben, and he flips the ball to Bartlett, who fires to Pena at first to complete the inning-ending double play. Ben says, "I guess you were right."

Sometimes you get lucky like that. I knew what I was going to throw Berkman and what I wanted to him to do, then I executed my pitch. Figuring out little ways to make hitters do things is one of the challenges of pitching and one of the elements that makes pitching so much fun.

After a shaky start, I feel good about getting out of the first having given up just one run, particularly considering that I faced Cano. Like I said, he's been wearing me out. On July 16 at Yankee Stadium, he homered off me in the sixth inning on a backdoor cutter that I still consider to be one of the best pitches I've thrown all year. Still, he managed to square it up, and he hit a scud about two feet off the ground over the center-field wall. I didn't think it would go out because it was hit so low. I'm telling you, that Cano is some kind of hitter.

After Colin Curtis lines out to Pena at first for the first out in the seventh, Joe comes out and gets me. We're leading 2–1 when Chad Qualls comes in to face Derek Jeter, and that's when the fun begins.

Qualls throws an inside pitch that appears to hit the knob of Jeter's bat. Not only does it look that way, but you can hear a sound like a ball hitting a bat. To everybody on our bench the ball appears to have hit the bat and rolled into fair play as a little ground ball before being converted into the second out of the inning. Instead, Jeter acts as if the ball hit him, and home-plate umpire Lance Barksdale buys the performance and awards Jeter first base.

We can't believe the call. I don't know how an umpire's eyes can be good enough to differentiate between the ball hitting a batter's hand or the bat, and I think the sound of ball on wood is a pretty compelling argument that Jeter's bat hit the ball. We think the play should be reversed based on these factors, but it isn't.

We start jawing with Barksdale. Garza and Price are going nuts, and both of them come close to getting kicked out of the game. I mean, we're trying anything we can to get outs, and we know that was an out. Then again, Jeter did a great job of acting. He must have had some acting classes; after all, during the off-season he was in that Will Ferrell movie, "The Other Guys." I think he did the right thing for his own team, though.

Joe argues the play, and later, when we watch the replays, they validate our point of view, which doesn't help Maddon a lick. He gets ejected. Granderson then steps to the plate and jacks his eighteenth homer of the season to put the Yankees up 3–2.

Luckily, Dan Johnson steps up to be the man—again!

Johnson hit what is still perceived to be the most important hit in Rays team history on September 9, 2008, against the Red Sox at Fenway Park. That was the night he hit a game-tying, pinch-hit home run against Jonathan Papelbon in the ninth inning to send the game into extra innings. We won that game 5–4 and seemed to have the Red Sox on the run after that.

Johnson played for the Yokohoma Stars in Japan during the 2009 season, then returned to the United States and the Rays' organization this year with an appreciation for a fair strike zone. In Japan, he felt like every time he took a pitch the umpires would call it a strike.

Johnson crushed the ball at Durham this season, hitting .332 with 30 home runs and 95 RBIs. He joined us on August 2 and hit the walk-off homer against the Red Sox on August 28, but he hasn't limited his heroics to the Red Sox this year. Prior to Jeter's theatrics, Johnson hit a two-run homer off Phil Hughes in the fifth, and now, after we've fallen behind again, he follows up with another two-run homer in the seventh off Hughes. Grant Balfour pitches a scoreless eighth and Rafael Soriano a scoreless ninth to preserve our 4–3 win while picking up his forty-third save.

Johnson's at-bat was unbelievable—one of the most special moments of the year. Johnson has just been so good in the clutch for us, and hitting two two-run home runs to win the game is truly something special. He is the hero tonight. While listening to the postgame show later, I learn that he's hit five game-winning homers on September 15, so I guess next September 15 we should make sure he's in the lineup.

After the game, Jeter's acting comes under more scrutiny. I think he says all the right things when he tells reporters:

"It's part of the game. I've been hit before and they said I wasn't hit. My job is to get on base, and fortunately for us it paid off at the time. I'm sure it would have been a bigger story if we would have won that game."

The incident brings out some funny comments, too, including one from Joe:

"There are several thespians throughout baseball. I thought Derek did a great job, and again, I applaud it, because I wish our guys would do the same thing."

The next day, Jeter continues to catch a lot of crap, mostly because the majority of baseball fans either hate the Yankees or love them. If you hate the Yankees, you're saying, "Jeter's a cheater," but if you love the Yankees, you're thinking what a good play that was. He essentially admitted that the ball hit the bat and the umpire told him to go to first, and he wasn't going to complain about it. I think any other player in that situation would have done the same thing.

Jeter's play aside, we did what we had to do against the Yankees by taking two out of three at home to move half a game in front in the American League East. But nobody on the team believes we're home free. There's a lot of baseball left in this pennant race.

Standings on September 15

Tm	W	L	GB
TBR	88	57	--
NYY	88	58	0.5
BOS	82	64	6.5
TOR	73	73	15.5
BAL	58	88	30.5

Curveball

SEVEN
September 16–19

After three days of battling the Yankees, we get an off-day on the Thursday prior to starting a weekend series against the Angels.

The Tampa Bay area is not a bad place to enjoy an off-day. There are a lot of things to do in the area, particularly if you like to be outdoors. I enjoy playing golf, and there are plenty of nice courses in the area, so sometimes during the season I'll sneak out for a round on an off-day. But the early part of this day starts with family time. My wife and I take the kids to Clearwater Beach, which is close to where we live. Later I head to a charity poker tournament at Derby Lane.

Some people think I must be some kind of gambling expert or card shark because I lived in Las Vegas for five years, but the truth is that I didn't frequent the casinos much. There's so much to do outside the Strip—most especially, in my case, the amazing golf courses that surround Vegas. Most people go to Vegas to gamble, see the shows, drink, and have a good time, but when I lived there the only time I went to the Strip was to watch a show or when buddies came to town.

I'm not much of a poker player, but I go to this Derby Lane event to have fun and to help raise money for the charity. Being a celebrity guest has its perks—they give me free chips to play Texas hold 'em. I prefer Black Jack and craps on those rare occasions when I do gamble, but since Texas hold 'em is the game of the hour, I decide just to have some fun playing with the guests, many of whom are there hoping to win big money. A good or lucky player could take home as much as fifteen grand this day. For the first hour I play aggressively, staying in the game with cards like a 3 and an 8 in the hole, cards I would fold with if I were betting my own money. One guy at the table turns out to be a professional poker player, and when I call him on one hand, going all in, he says, "I can't believe you called me. I went to the World Series of Poker." I say, "I don't care who you are, I'm still going to call you," then I proceed to get lucky with the river card (the last of the five community cards to be flopped by the dealer) and end up beating him. He starts getting mad, then calls me all in on the next hand and ends up beating me. He's taking the game pretty seriously, but afterwards he gets a laugh from it.

Throughout my day off, I feel a sense of relief about being finished with the Yankees for the time being. You look forward to a series like that, but it takes a lot out of you, and I hope we don't have a letdown after playing them. You simply can't afford a letdown in the major leagues, because there are just too many good players on every team. You have to be at your best every night or you're going to get your butts handed to you. Most every player in the majors has been, at one time or another, the biggest and best player in their little corner of the world. You realize that when you get to the big leagues—particularly if you are a pitcher. In the minor leagues you can get away with mistakes, but those same mistakes end up in the seats in the major leagues.

Knowing we'll be playing the Yankees again next week, we have to be concerned, too, about the effect that looking ahead to that series could have on our team during the intervening series. Returning to work on Friday, we all know we have to get back down to business. The Angels are in St. Petersburg, and the Angels are not a team to be taken lightly.

We're used to playing close games, which is a good thing given the nature of playoff baseball. If you're used to playing close games, you are better conditioned to play in the postseason, and the Rays are built to play close games. Everything this team has done since the new ownership group took over has been built around a foundation of strong starting pitching, and we have excellent defenders behind us. All of the starters—myself included—will bitch from time to time about not getting the run support we need, but one thing anybody criticizing our offense needs to remember is that nobody takes the field for our team if they can't play defense. Any deficiencies we might have on offense are offset by the highlight films that play out every night on defense.

Management has put our starting rotation in a position to succeed. They have propped us up to be the rock stars of the team, so it's up to us to carry the team into the sixth inning and beyond if we possibly can. If we are able to keep the team in the game through six or seven innings, we have a good chance of winning. We can usually find a way to scrape out a run or two in the late innings, and once our starters leave, we have a good bullpen, which is made even better because the starters kill so many innings.

Any reliever should want to come to the Rays, because he will be put in a position to succeed by the number of innings logged by our starting staff. A lot of relievers get worn out over the course of a season because they are asked to cover too many innings. Most all of the relievers in our bullpen are able to assume fairly defined roles, and when we starters are doing our jobs, the relievers get to stay inside their comfort zones.

All of us starters pride ourselves on getting deep into a game. Of course there will be starts when we don't pitch well and last only four or five innings—that's why we have four other starters backing us up. One good thing about our starting staff is that we've done a great job the last three or four years, so if somebody has a bad game, the next guy is going to have a great game, giving the bullpen the rest they need. We pride ourselves on that. We compete with each other to see how deep we can go, and we feed off each other. I think that's part of our recipe for success.

Given the way we are built, we have a lot of confidence going into the late innings if we haven't already been blown out of the game, which doesn't happen often.

Our first game against the Angels is another close one. Wade Davis starts and pitches well, allowing two runs and striking out eight in six innings. Dan Haren starts for the Angels, and he's tough. Joe Maddon will best describe what Haren does on the mound this day when, in postgame comments, Maddon says, "It looked like badminton. His ball must have been moving all over the place."

Of course, a discomforting element of playing close games is that the margin of error is so small. The smallest mistake can derail a close game, and that's exactly what happens in the bottom of the eighth, right when everything seemed to be falling into place for us. Haren and Davis have both left the game by the time we come to bat in the bottom of the eighth with the score tied at 3. Michael Kohn comes on to pitch for the Angels, and John Jaso greets the right-hander with a single through the right side of the infield. Desmond Jennings then enters the game to pinch run for Jaso. Ben Zobrist moves him to second base with a sacrifice bunt, and Carl Crawford walks, and suddenly we're in business, with Evan Longoria stepping to the plate fishing for his hundredth RBI of the season.

Everything looks pre-ordained at this point. Longo will get his benchmark RBI, we'll take a 4–3 lead, and Rafael Soriano will come in to pitch the ninth, game over. Only the game takes an odd turn.

Desmond is still feeling his way around the big leagues, and when you're not playing every day, it's hard to come up to the majors and remain as aggressive as you were in the minor leagues. I've watched a lot of base runners, and the good ones have a fearlessness that is almost instinctive. It's a catch-me-if-you-can attitude, and I believe you have to be in there every day to develop that, no matter how fast you are.

Stealing third can be easy for guys like C.C. and Jennings, except that Jennings is in that kind of insecure mode from not play-ing enough. Desmond has a green light, which means that he, like

September 16-19 / 87

most anybody else on the team who can run, has permission to run whenever he wants. Joe likes it that way. He wants his base runners to be aggressive due to all the positive things it can bring to an offense and all the negative things it brings to the defense. Unfortunately for Jennings—and for us—Kohn takes an extra look at second base the instant Desmond decides to break for third. The Angels nail him, and that proves to be a killer for us.

I feel bad for Jennings. He's a good kid, and I think he's going to be a good player. There are just times when inexperience can hurt you.

Desmond getting thrown out initiates a series of events that might not have happened had he stayed on second or made it safely to third. C.C. goes to second while Desmond is being tagged out, so the Angels intentionally walk Longo. Matt Joyce then walks to load the bases, and it appears that we might win despite that little smudge on the ledger, particularly since Dan Johnson is now stepping to the plate. Wednesday night's two-home-run performance remains fresh in my mind, and I wonder if he can do it again. But home-plate umpire Phil Cuzzi calls Johnson out looking to end the inning.

Having failed to grab the lead, Joe goes to Dan Wheeler instead of Soriano.

Wheels has already had a bad week, dating back to Tuesday night when Jorge Posada touched him for the game winner. When it comes to the mental game of baseball, finding your way out of a bad streak is harder than keeping a hot streak going. A good outing, gives you something to build on, whereas all you can do after a bad outing is review your mistakes and try not to let the negativity and the doubt get into your mind. I can empathize with Dan.

Brandon Wood leads off the ninth for California. He takes ball one, then connects on Wheels' second pitch, depositing a fastball into the left-field stands to give the Angels a 4–3 lead. And that's that.

Anytime something like that happens, watching the scoreboard feels like water torture. Drip, drip, drip, the Yankees win 4–3 over the Orioles on Alex Rodriguez's three-run homer in the ninth, and once again we're a half game out of first place.

As if anybody needs more proof that C.C. is one of the best

players in baseball, he hits his thirteenth triple of the season in the sixth inning of Friday night's game, making him the third player in the last 75 years to hit 90 triples over a seven-year span. Stan Musial and Lance Johnson were the only other players to do so.

David Price starts Saturday night's game. True to form, he continues to post zeroes on the scoreboard—six of them over the first six innings, to be exact. He allows just one hit over the first six, and we enter the seventh leading 2–0. Results notwithstanding, I think Price had much better stuff on Monday night against the Yankees, when his fastball was overpowering.

Price has become a much better pitcher. We work together frequently between starts, playing catch and experimenting with how to throw different pitches. He sees what works for me, and I see what works for him. We might compare notes or offer each other suggestions on what might make this pitch or that pitch work better. All of the catchers know what our pitches look like, but most of the pitchers on our team do, too. We help each other as much as we can.

Lately I've been working with him between starts on his changeup. He had been throwing a four-seam change and trying to slow it down a little bit to make a greater contrast with his fastball, but I've taught him how to throw a two-seam change and to throw it a little bit harder. He starts getting a little extra movement when he throws his changeup at 84 MPH, and against the Angels tonight he throws a couple of two-seamers that drop off the table. They're beauties. If he can have a changeup like that and throw his fastball at 98 MPH with a little bit of a curve, he's unhittable, especially for left-handers. When he came back to the dugout after breaking out that changeup in the first inning tonight, you could tell he felt pretty good about it.

He's learning every day, just like everybody else is. He's had great success, and every start he's trying to learn more. But against the Angels, we're all reminded once again that sometimes luck factors into the equation.

After his great showing through the first six innings, he walks Mike Napoli with one out in the seventh. Howie Kendrick follows with an infield hit, then Juan Rivera runs into Price's first pitch and homers to right-center field to give the Angels a 3–2 lead. That leads to a bizarre finish.

We're down to our final two outs against Fernando Rodney, who is out there throwing 99 MPH. He throws gas, and he's got an 82 MPH changeup to go with his fastball. That's a 16– to 18–MPH difference, which can really mess with a hitter's head. He's got all the physical tools and pitches, but we've had some success against him in the past. We know that if we stay patient with him, good things might happen—and they do. Johnson gets us started when he swings at a changeup with two outs. He makes contact, but barely. Our very own Mr. September, fresh off a two-home-run game, hits a full-swing dribbler bunt right down the third-base line and somehow legs it out. Johnson has given us enough with his legs at this point, so Jennings enters the game as a pinch runner and moves to third on a single by Matt Joyce before scoring on a single by Carlos Pena. That sends the game into extra innings, where, ironically, the baseball gods once again demonstrate their fickle nature. They can give and they also can take away. Friday night's hero, Wood, makes a throwing error in the bottom of the tenth on a ball hit by Willy Aybar to give us a walk-off 4–3 win at the Trop. Of course, the Yankees win, too, so we're still a half game out.

You have to have some luck. You need just enough runs to win the game, and how you get them doesn't matter. All year we've been winning the one-run and extra-inning games. In the eighth and ninth innings, I think we're an all-star team.

A cool side note from tonight's win is that it gives the Rays 270 wins over the last three seasons—90 wins per year since 2008. That makes us the fourth team all-time to average ninety-plus wins over three consecutive seasons after averaging ninety or more losses for three consecutive seasons. When I see something like that, my chest fills with a little bit of pride at how far we've come since I've been here.

Scott Kazmir starts for the Angels in the series finale on Sunday.

When Kaz got traded to the Angels late in the 2009 season, everybody viewed the move as an indication that our management had given up on the season. In reality, they were doing two things.

They brought in some younger players in the trade—including Sean Rodriguez—and they dumped Kaz's salary. A franchise like Tampa Bay can't afford to make many mistakes by giving a player too much money, particularly when that player struggles. Kaz had a couple of good starts before the trade, but he hadn't been the same dominating pitcher in 2009 that he had been before. None of us felt like the club had given up by making the trade. We understood what the ownership was trying to do, keeping young players and trading away—or not re-signing—players making really good money. You don't necessarily have to like a move the club makes, but you can respect what they're doing and why they're doing it. Kaz had a contract that paid him $8 million for 2010 and $12 million for 2011. Management had an opportunity to knock $20 million off the payroll, and they felt they could get more value spending that money elsewhere.

Nevertheless, seeing him in the uniform of another team feels a bit strange after having him for a teammate for so long.

Kaz played a big part in all the success we had over the previous three or four years. When I got called up to the major leagues, Kaz was already on the team. We were both young, and it was tough on him to be called up as the ace of the staff. We had guys rotating in and out of the starting rotation, and there were no other pitchers on the staff that he could really emulate. He did a lot of good things for us. He threw hard, 97–98 MPH from the left side.

He's struggled for the Angels this season, and he struggled here most of last year, which has been strange to witness because I saw him when he could dominate a game. I don't know what has happened to him. It's possible that he's hurt, but I have no clue. I know that hitters have been fouling off a lot of his pitches, and that leads to large pitch counts. When you're on the mound and that happens, you look around and suddenly you've got ninety to a hundred pitches and it's just the fifth inning. I've seen that happen to Price, too. When he's throwing 96 MPH he can have 12–pitch at-bats, 10–pitch at-bats, because his stuff is almost overly nasty. The hitters just nick a pitch instead of putting the ball into play, and next thing you know he has a 10–pitch at-bat going, and pretty soon the pitch count becomes a factor.

I faced Kaz on August 23 in Anaheim and got the win. In his last two starts against us, both in Anaheim, he has gone 0–2 with a

5.23 ERA. Today is his first start at Tropicana Field since getting traded. Kaz brings back some old memories by holding us to one run over five innings to lead the Angels' 6–3 win. He needs 103 pitches to get through five, though. It's hard to figure out what's going on with Kaz, but I find myself thinking, "Good for him," since we'd all like to see him start pitching the way we know he can.

Through the last five games, it seems like we've been on the edge of our seats or anxiously pacing the length of the dugout. If we make an out, or our defense comes in at the end of an inning after shutting them out, we're all there giving everybody high fives. We're really amped up. You can feel the playoff atmosphere and how bad we want to win this thing. Everybody knows how much each and every inning and every single at-bat matters. We still goof around in the dugout, but lately everything's been more serious than funny. Partly that's because everybody is really concentrating on what's happening in the games. We know the playoffs are right around the corner. The intensity level is dialed up and we're starting to get those butterflies.

Following Sunday's game, we have another themed road trip heading into our four-game series against the Yankees in New York.

Joe comes up with these themed trips to help us stay loose. They can be silly—even corny, but they have served their purpose since we started doing them a couple of years ago.

The idea is to dress up in attire that fits the theme of the road trip. Past themes have included all-white, Ed Hardy, urban cowboy, and hockey jerseys, to name a few. After getting beat by the Angels in the final game of the series, we embark on the "Loudmouth Pants Rowland road trip."

Joe started getting into Clarence "Pants" Rowland shortly after we got no-hit for the second time this season. First, Dallas Braden pitched a perfect game against us on Mother's Day at Oakland on May 9. I remember the game well—I got the loss. Then Edwin Jackson pitched a no-hitter against us on June 25 at Tropicana Field. Jack's game was a testament to what a strong pitcher he is. He walked eight and threw 149 pitches—of which only 79 were strikes—and still came away with the no-no.

Joe, who always manages to find a silver lining in everything, somehow discovered that the 1917 Chicago White Sox were the only team in baseball history to get no-hit twice during the regular season and still win the World Series. Rowland managed that club, so Joe became a Pants fan. If you go into his office, you can see a framed 8 x 10 black and white glossy of Pants Rowland on his desk. Loudmouth Golf contributed the pants for the trip, which make us look like a group of extras for a "Caddyshack" casting call.

A loss can be especially hard to take this late in the year. Right after Sunday's game, there is about twenty minutes of silence. Nobody wants to laugh about anything or talk about anything. But we just have to remember that we have the second-best record in baseball and we're only a half game back in the standings. So we do these themed road trips, and win or lose, we follow through. Are these trips stupid and silly? You bet they are. And when you start to dress up like that after losing, the whole thing feels even more stupid. Everybody looks particularly ridiculous for this trip, but there is a lot of laughter, and pretty soon we've all forgotten our loss to the Angels. It definitely helps a little bit. It gets our minds off baseball. There have been times when we probably shouldn't have done the themed trip, but Joe stays consistent with it. All he cares about is keeping us loose, relaxed, and having fun, and today, as usual, Joe's mission is accomplished.

Another way guys are staying loose these days is playing fantasy football, which is kind of funny when you consider we're always dealing with fans asking us to do well because "you're on my fantasy team." We usually laugh about that. To be honest, I don't really know what is good for a fantasy baseball team. Wins and strikeouts are good, I guess, but I don't know what the point system is or how you keep score.

When it comes to fantasy football, however, I'm obsessed with it. I'm playing in a league with a lot of the guys on the team including Rocco Baldelli, Kelly Shoppach, B.J. Upton, Longoria, Randy Choate, Jeff Niemann, Gabe Kapler, J.P. Howell, and Lance Cormier, to name a few. We've had a lot of fun with it so far.

There are no TVs on the charter flight to New York, which gets everyone grumbling because we wanted to watch the games and find out how the players on our teams have done. We end up asking the co-pilot to call in and ask for the scores. The big game was between the Colts and the Giants—Peyton Manning vs. Eli Manning, brother vs. brother. Peyton's on my team. The 4 o'clock games are still going on, so the co-pilot is announcing the scores over the PA and everyone is going nuts. To play fantasy football and talk some trash with these guys is a lot of fun.

Standings on September 19

Tm	W	L	GB
NYY	90	59	--
TBR	89	59	0.5
BOS	83	66	7.0
TOR	75	74	15.0
BAL	59	90	31.0

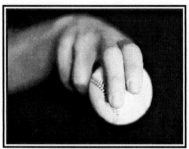

Two-seam fastball

EIGHT
September 20-23

YOU WANT TO MAKE SURE YOU'RE DOING all the little things right when you're on the mound. If you lose a game because you're not pitching well, that's one thing. But if you lose by doing something stupid or not preparing well, that's another. That will eat you up.

One aspect of game management is controlling the other team's running game. I've worked hard at finding ways to accomplish that, and it's paid off for me.

Keeping runners close isn't only about preventing opposing runners from stealing bases. Keeping them close can also prevent them from going from first to third on a single or from first to home on a double. Thus, keeping runners close can easily make the difference between winning and losing.

A big part of my success in keeping runners close can be attributed to what I do when I'm in the stretch. Most right-handed pitchers just peer over their left shoulder to see what the base runner is doing. I bend down and make a full turn toward the base before I come set. Dick Bosman taught me this technique.

Bos, who pitched in the major leagues for eleven seasons—mostly for the old Washington Senators—helped me a lot early in my professional career as my pitching coach. He always preached the importance of controlling the running game and being able to identify how big a lead the runner has over at first base. Employing Bos's technique allows me to use both eyes to judge the distance of the runner's lead. Using both eyes gives you depth perception. After you've come set, you can take another look over at first and use your peripheral vision, which allows you to pick up movement. Getting used to that was a little difficult at first, which might explain why other pitchers don't use the technique, but I've been doing it so long now—since 2001—that it has become routine to me. I don't know anything different.

Another part of the equation comes prior to each game, when I examine the cutout at first base. The cutout is the arc cut into the infield grass or turf at each base, and the point where the arc of the first-base cutout meets the path between first and second base is usually approximately 12 feet from first base. Knowing how big the cutout is allows me to understand how large a lead the runner has. If the lead isn't big, I simply make my pitch to the plate.

There's not a lot the other team can do about my motion. If a runner takes a big lead, there's a good chance I'm going to pick him off. Their only recourse for combating what I do is not to take a big lead, and if they do that, I've won the battle.

The Yankees aren't going to steal a lot of bases, but the way they hit makes it critical to do all the little things right. Since you know they are going to get their hits, you don't want to help them out by giving them anything else.

Facing any major-league lineup is challenging enough, but facing the Yankees or Red Sox is altogether different. All teams have great players, but any one of the guys hitting one through nine in the Yankees and Red Sox batting orders could hit in the three- or five-hole on another team. One through nine, both teams have stacked lineups.

Both teams go out and spend a lot of money to get really good players, and that's one of the biggest challenges of playing in the

American League East. You face teams like Boston and New York, and one through nine you don't have a break—none. I remember at one point Robinson Cano was hitting in the ninth spot for the Yankees. Are you kidding me? He's not a nine hitter. As I've previously stated, I think he's one of the toughest outs in the big leagues. Any pitcher will tell you that. And there he was at one point hitting ninth for the Yankees. There are times when you look at that lineup and think to yourself, "This is going to be a tough day to go get those guys." Aside from the inherent ration of anxiety I feel when waiting to pitch against the Yankees or Red Sox, I usually find myself eager to make the start. The competitive part of me wants to see how I stack up against the best, and both of those teams are studded with All-Stars and a few future Hall of Famers.

While I have a high opinion of the hitters on the Yankees and Red Sox, I try to grind it out every night no matter who I'm pitching against. I treat every team as if they are the best in the league. There are no teams in the big leagues that I or any other pitcher can afford to take lightly. That's why it's the big leagues. There are no levels higher than this level, and you have to remember that. They want to hit you as bad as you want to strike them out.

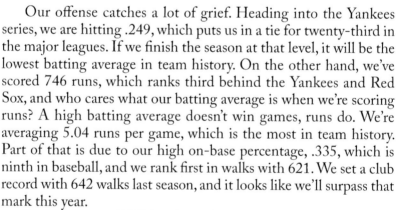

Our offense catches a lot of grief. Heading into the Yankees series, we are hitting .249, which puts us in a tie for twenty-third in the major leagues. If we finish the season at that level, it will be the lowest batting average in team history. On the other hand, we've scored 746 runs, which ranks third behind the Yankees and Red Sox, and who cares what our batting average is when we're scoring runs? A high batting average doesn't win games, runs do. We're averaging 5.04 runs per game, which is the most in team history. Part of that is due to our high on-base percentage, .335, which is ninth in baseball, and we rank first in walks with 621. We set a club record with 642 walks last season, and it looks like we'll surpass that mark this year.

In my opinion, OPS (on-base plus slugging) works better than batting average for indicating how well a player or an offense is doing. An OPS adds a hitter's or a team's on-base percentage to his slugging percentage (total bases divided by number of at-bats) to get a combined statistic. It's a relatively new stat, much like WHIP for pitchers. WHIP is an acronym for walks and hits per inning pitched, and you calculate it by adding the hits and walks allowed and then dividing that total by the number of innings pitched. Obviously, the lower a pitcher's WHIP, the better he is performing. I think OPS and WHIP are pretty good stats for measuring a player's value.

Whatever the stats might suggest about our team, we are thirty games over .500 heading into the Yankees series, and that's a pretty strong bottom line.

We've got 14 games remaining in the season, and we're a half game behind the Yankees, so these are important games. But you can't go out there with a football mentality letting your emotions get the best of you. Baseball is best played on an even keel, so it's kind of a balancing act when you play games like these against the Yankees. You know they are important, and you have to treat them as such, but all of the games we play are important. They all count the same, and when you treat one game as if it's more important than the others, that's when you set yourself up for trouble.

Whether we win the division or not, we appear to be a lock for the playoffs. I don't really want to look backward or forward, I need to stay in the moment. But I can't help reflecting just a little bit. I know, as does everybody on this team, that next year is racing toward us like a rocket. And next season is going to be different. A lot of the players from this team won't be here. So we march forward trying to make the most of the time we have left. We want to win the division, and we want to win the World Series to have something to show for the time we played together. This is a special group.

Almost as a reminder of what this group is facing, Stu Sternberg, the principal owner of the team, is on hand prior to the game. He lives in the New York area, so he comes to most of our games in New York. He's a great owner, and he's always been candid when talking about the team, what it needs to do to be financially successful, and the future of baseball in the Tampa Bay area. I find it odd that a lot of people believe an owner should just throw money into a team in order to win without any regard to whether they lose money or not. While that sounds good in principle, as if the owner of a team is just a sportsman who doesn't worry about making money, the owners of all these franchises want to make money, too. Anybody who is a businessman wants to make money, and they most certainly don't want to lose money. Stu is passionate about baseball, and I think that while he's a businessman, his main reason for wanting the team to be profitable is so that he can use those profits to improve the team. You can't fault him for not wanting to lose money while following his passion.

During Stu's remarks, he reiterates his spring training message, saying that next year's payroll will be reduced even if we go deep into the playoffs. According to Stu, the financial gains made from a postseason run include a boost in season-ticket sales the following season. He witnessed that after the 2008 season, but season-ticket sales dropped again in 2009, and he isn't optimistic that the team will enjoy the same kind of boost in season-ticket sales in 2011 that they experienced after 2008. Keeping his sense of humor, he adds, "Unfortunately there's nothing that can change that between now and April unless Joe Maddon hits the lottery and wants to donate it."

Our payroll hit $72 million this season, and some are saying that the 2011 payroll will be half that. Such speculation adds even more resolve to those of us inside the clubhouse. We need to get the job done this season.

Comparisons between the Yankees and us are inevitable at the beginning of the series. The Yankees are portrayed as a team with worlds of experience, but long in the tooth and one step away from retirement. We're portrayed as the team having a perpetual fountain of youth but lacking the necessary experience to go all the way. That has led to speculation about how each of our teams is going to play things down the stretch. Due to the Yankees' age, everybody is starting to talk about the prospect of them resting their players a lot during the final weeks so they will be fresh for the playoffs. I think most of that talk is pretty ridiculous. I can't see Derek Jeter, Mariano Rivera, or Jorge Posada needing that rest. They are true professionals. Once the playoffs start, they won't need anybody to show them how to get ready or how to get up. They'll be just where they need to be. Being a professional is all about knowing what needs to get done and doing it.

We play the opening game of the series on September 20 with 47,437 watching at Yankee Stadium. Ever since the Yankees moved to the new Yankee Stadium, I think the place has had a totally different vibe, which has been a good thing for us based on our team's history at the original Yankee Stadium.

The Rays played 91 games at the original Yankee Stadium and went 26–65. That's a winning percentage of .286. Personally, I got a rude introduction to the old Yankee Stadium administered by Johnny Damon on July 30, 2006. He hit two two-run homers off me in a 4–2 Yankees win on a Sunday afternoon. I only allowed four hits that day. On another Sunday afternoon in July 2007, they scored 10 runs on me in 3⅓ innings. But I parted on good terms with the old stadium on September 13, 2008, when I pitched my final game there. I held the Yankees to no runs on five hits in eight innings during the first game of a Saturday double-header to pick up the win. All told, I went 1–3 with a 6.25 ERA in five starts at "The House that Ruth Built."

The new stadium looks almost identical when you're out on the field, but it's a lot different. While the new stadium has all the bells and whistles any fan could dream about a ballpark having, the park lost something in the way of ambiance. The other park had so much history going for it, which created an aura. Every little nook and cranny throughout the building had some kind of story attached to it. Ticket prices went up at the new park, which priced out a lot of the regulars who had been attending the games for so many years. But Yankee fans are Yankee fans and they will show no matter which stadium it is. The old park was just that, old—concrete gets old, steel rusts, and various features of the park were outdated. Yankee Stadium had lived a good life, and it was time to move on, nostalgia or not. And the Yankees did pretty well in their first year at the new stadium, since they went to the World Series and won.

Getting to the World Series is what everybody plays for, which brings to mind another topic that won't go away—and that is the notion that the Yankees wouldn't mind if they were the Wild Card team this season. It's looking like the Rangers will be the team that the winner of the East will have to play in the first round, and the Twins will be the team the Wild Card plays. Speculation continues that the Yankees would rather avoid facing Cliff Lee in a five-game series. We'll see what happens.

The Yankees hardly look like a team content to be the Wild Card when they beat us 8-6 in Monday's opener.

Communication between the bench and the bullpen becomes a part of the story in this loss. After we score four runs in the sixth to tie the game at 4–4, the Yankees answer with three consecutive singles off Matt Garza in the bottom half of the inning to take a one-run lead. With Curtis Granderson due up next, Joe goes out to get Garza, thinking he has lefty Randy Choate warmed up to face the left-handed hitting Granderson. Instead, when Joe leaves the dugout, he sees Grant Balfour heading for the mound to enter the game.

The problem actually stems from a conversation between Joe and our pitching coach, Jim Hickey. Joe says later he had talked to Hick about several different scenarios when discussing how they were going to use the bullpen, which is where the confusion entered the picture. In the confusion, Balfour became the only guy warming up in that situation.

The confusion ended up hurting us, too. You want a left-hander to face Granderson, who does really well against right-handers. Granderson got ahead in the count 2–1 before re-routing one of Grant's fastballs up in the strike zone for a three-run home run, and that pretty much was the game at that point.

All of a sudden, our starting pitching is beginning to look suspect.

Garza has lost for the second time in his last three starts and allowed six or more runs and eight or more hits for the third consecutive start. Combine that with what I've been doing lately and what Jeff Niemann has been doing, and you can see that selecting our rotation for the playoffs is going to be more difficult than it should have been. I expect to be on the playoff roster, but a manager has to pick his best players. If Joe had to pick his playoff rotation for the first round right now, there would at least be some dialogue about me not being in the mix.

Longoria has two RBIs in our loss, which gives him back-to-back 100–RBI seasons. Had he not been injured at the end of his rookie season in 2008, it's likely he would have had three consecutive 100–RBI seasons; he finished that season with 85 in 122 games. You can't put somebody in the Hall of Fame after three seasons, but Lango certainly looks on track to waltz right into Cooperstown once he retires. He does it all, and he handles being a star well.

The loss to the Yankees puts us 1 ½ games back with the third-best record in the majors behind the Yankees and Twins.

On Tuesday morning I get up around 9 and follow my usual routine for the days that I pitch. I walk around New York City and find a place to eat breakfast. Even though New York is a big baseball city, I can walk around without anybody noticing me other than the autograph seekers who stand outside the hotel waiting for players. We call them "graphers." Those guys obviously recognize me, because they want me to sign the stack of cards and photos they carry in their briefcases. But I'm not a Derek Jeter or an Alex Rodriguez, so the rest of New York doesn't recognize me when I'm walking around the streets.

A lot of times while I'm walking, I'll think about what I'm going to do that night when I pitch. This time I think about throwing a changeup on the first pitch to Jeter to get my changeup into their minds. If they're sitting on changeup, that means I'm definitely getting into their heads. That makes my fastball that much better, and that in turn makes my breaking ball that much better. Obviously my changeup is my best pitch, and it's still going to be my best pitch. My fastball is always going to be the pitch I throw the most, but if they're sitting on my changeup, I can sneak some fastballs by them. Even if you're sitting on changeup, it's still not an easy pitch to hit. The guys joke around with me in the dugout after each inning that it seems like I throw my changeup harder with my body than I do my fastball. I like giving that impression, because I know that does not feel good to a hitter.

I don't want to get too carried away with doing things differently against the Yankees, though. They are such good hitters that no matter what I throw they will stick with their approach. If I get too far outside my element, I might not do well.

I look forward to making this start. It will be one of the coolest of my career because of the atmosphere. You work to be in situations like this, pitching against the Yankees late in the season with the pennant on the line. We'll put a lot of pressure on the Yankees if we can split or take the series, because we'll then be going home for two series before finishing on the road against Kansas City, while the Yankees have to play the Red Sox six more games this season.

The Yankees saw me last Wednesday when I got a no-decision, but I put forth a quality start that night. Facing a team again so soon can present some problems, but it hasn't been much of a problem for me in the past. I've always felt that if I can execute my pitches, I'm able to beat any team. Hitters will tell you that the hardest thing there is to do is hit a baseball. You've got a round ball and a round bat, and you're trying to square a ball up. That's a tall order.

Unfortunately, I get out of the gates slowly. The second guy I face, Nick Swisher, hits a home run to right field. Then Posada adds an RBI single, Lance Berkman has a two-run double, and Granderson follows with an RBI single. Just like that, the Yankees are up 5–0 after one at-bat.

Not exactly the way I visualized the first inning, though I actually made some pretty good pitches. They just ended up getting the bat on those pitches and squeezing the ball through a hole. A-Rod hit a ball through the six-hole, and Posada hit a ball up the middle toward the second baseman that got through. I made a mistake to Berkman with two strikes, and he hit a line drive over B.J.'s head in center field. And that was pretty much all she wrote.

You can't give up five runs in the first to any team, particularly a team like the Yankees. You aren't doing your job when you do that. The only positive I can take from the outing is that I don't quit after they've clipped me pretty good. By the time I get Brett Gardner looking at strike three to end the first, I've thrown 42 pitches.

Experiencing that kind of first inning can send you into full panic mode. You don't know what to do. I can't just pack it in, though. It's tough sucking it up and hanging in there when you get off to a bad start, but there's plenty of game to go. I want to save the pen, and I know that if I don't get my act together Joe will pull me in the second inning. I saw those guys stretching in the bullpen. But I'm not about to give in. I figure I'm going to have to do something a little different. Knowing that we have two more games in the series, I don't want to be the cause of the bullpen being spent for those remaining games, so I shift into full-scale survival mode and make adjustments.

I struggled with my fastball in the first, missing with a couple that really hurt me. So I begin to throw some curves for strikes, which helps me inch out of the hole I've dug myself into. I think I'll look back on this game and regret not making those adjustments earlier. Despite my high pitch count in the first, I manage to make it through 5 1/3 innings, giving up just two more hits, before I finally get the hook after a 104 pitches.

At the end of the night, we take our third straight loss, 8-3, allowing the Yankees to increase their lead over us to 2 1/2 games.

A funny little incident occurs in the bottom of the third inning, and it comes almost a week after the Jeter controversy stemming from his not really getting hit by a pitch. Jeter isn't the star of this one, though. Instead it's Posada, enter stage left.

There are two outs in the inning and I'm ahead in the count 0–2 to Posada when I throw a low curveball that arrives around his ankles. Home-plate umpire Mike Everitt surmises that the ball hits Posada, who happily takes his base.

Joe goes out to discuss the matter with Everitt, but this time he doesn't get tossed like he did while arguing the merits of Jeter's acting skills last week. The replays show that Posada didn't get hit by the pitch, but it doesn't matter because I get the next hitter, Berkman, to line out to first, ending the inning.

Leave it to Joe to put it into proper perspective. When he's asked about the play after the game, he notes, "We're in New York. It's the theater district. Bully for them."

After my start, the scrutinizing of our starting pitching intensifies. Niemann, Garza, and I have not done anything in the last three games to change the perception that all three of us are limping home. All of us would acknowledge that we have hit a bump in the road and we're in a rut, no doubt. But we don't lack for confidence. Overall, the starting rotation did a phenomenal job for the first 5 ½ months of the season. Now, any problems the team is having are attributed to the starting pitching. If you believed everything that is written or said, you would be convinced that we are the proverbial rowboat bailing water. But we'll take the blame on our shoulders, and over the next couple of weeks we have to bear down and do well. The playoffs are coming. We know we have to get ourselves right. I believe in my abilities, and I believe in the abilities of the other guys, so I think we're going to be just fine.

My thirteenth loss of the season drops us to 0–2 in our big series and causes a lot of baseball experts to concede the division to the Yankees. If they want to do that, that's their business, but we're not going anywhere, and the Yankees know that. Phil Hughes started for the Yankees against me, and he escaped some jams. We could easily have come back. They know that and we know that. They know what we have over here. We put on a nice little display at home against them, winning two of three. They know we're good enough to win the division.

I think a lot of the reporters put too much emphasis on what certain people are or aren't doing. The bottom line is that we're the second-best team in the American League East, just 2 ½ games back from the best record in baseball. We've got all the confidence in the world to get this thing done.

And on the bright side, even though we lost, our magic number to make the playoffs gets reduced to six games Tuesday night, since Baltimore takes it to Boston 9–1.

We're all pretty excited about being that close to clinching. We sit there and watch the Twins celebrate clinching the American League Central. That gets us all to start talking about how we're going to celebrate this year when that time comes. In 2008 we celebrated for the first time, and that was really exciting. We've got a good group of guys, and I think our celebrations are going to be pretty strong. We were new to celebrations in 2008, so it will be hard to top those. On the other hand, we know what we're doing now, so we're planning to basically go nuts. You don't get many opportunities to go to the playoffs. Some guys never go to the play-offs, let alone get a chance to go to the World Series. We're defi-nitely going to celebrate hard.

After what Garza and I did in the first two games, we need a lift from Wade Davis and David Price in the final two games of the series.

We get off to a good start in the third game. Longoria has a sacrifice fly in the first against Yankees starter A.J. Burnett to put us up 1–0. Meanwhile, Davis does not allow a hit in the first two innings. After retiring Berkman on a popup to start the bottom of the third, Davis walks Granderson, then goes to 1–1 against Francisco Cervelli. That's when the skies open up and rain begins to soak Yankee Stadium. Davis has only thrown 33 pitches, but the way the rain is coming down, we all know he's finished for the night. Back in the old days, pitchers would sit out a rain delay and return to pitch later, but you never see that happen these days.

Once they start pulling the tarp over the infield, we head for the clubhouse to kill time, hoping all the while that we can some-how get the game in rather than having to play a double-header tomorrow. You never know how long a rain delay is going to last, and there's always a chance that you'll end up with a total washout. One major benefit of a new stadium like the one the Yankees play in, however, is that the drainage is first class. If it stops raining, the chances are good that we will play.

Different players do different things during a rain delay. A lot of the guys on the team have iPads, so "Words with Friends" is pretty popular during the downtime. Other guys play cards or just hang out and watch TV. Guys will do anything to keep busy. But staying ready during a rain delay is totally different for a starting pitcher. I know I'm not going to pitch and neither are the other starters, so we're just killing time. Position players and the bullpen guys can't check out, because at any minute, somebody can step into the clubhouse and tell them that play will resume in twenty min-utes. They just never know. This time the game doesn't recommence until 2 hours and 11 minutes has passed.

Jeremy Hellickson takes over for Davis when we resume play, and he pitches well.

Again, this kid doesn't act like a kid. He really has poise on the mound. He has never pitched in Yankee Stadium before, and suddenly here he is pitching at the sport's most famous venue in a crucial game of a pennant race. Yet his body language and mannerisms give the appearance of someone calmly playing catch at a company picnic.

During the delay, Hickey told Helly he'd be putting him in, and in true Hellickson style, there was little to no reaction. Just kind of like, "Okay."

He starts his outing by striking out Cervelli, then he strikes out Gardner to end the inning. Thankfully, our offense gets cranked up, too. After the rain delay our hitters start banging the ball all over the park. Our guys were crushing Burnett right out of the gates, then came the rain delay and now they have to throw their bullpen in there, and we just pretty much put them away.

Carl Crawford's RBI single in the fifth puts us up 2–0, then Berkman cuts that lead with a home run off Hellickson in the bottom half of the inning. Dan Johnson answers with his seventh home run of the season in the sixth. In the bottom of that inning, ARod gets an RBI single off Helly, but once again the offense comes to the rescue as Crawford and Longo hit back-to-back homers off Chad Gaudin with two outs in the seventh.

We add single runs in the eighth and ninth innings to come away 7–2 winners.

Helly ends up allowing just two earned runs on three hits in 3 ⅓ innings to pick up the win, which makes him the third pitcher in team history to begin his career 4–0—a short list that includes Tim Corcoran and me (we both did that in 2006). Choate, Balfour, Joaquin Benoit, and Chad Qualls clean up the final 3 ⅓ innings without allowing any further damage.

Seeing our offense come to life with twelve hits and seven walks is a good sign and brings renewed hope for things to come.

By winning we close the gap with the Yankees back to 1½ games, and we also see our magic number move to five games. That number could have been reduced to four, but the Red Sox beat the Orioles 6–1.

All our wins right now are big, and we will gladly take them any way we can get them. Just lately it seems as though wins have been harder to come by, though, so everybody is happy to see us take the lead and not let them come back. After the game, everybody's thoughts shift to the idea of gaining a split. That would be huge.

Everyone looks forward to the pitching matchup in the final game: David Price vs. CC Sabathia, Part II.

Given how Part I played out, a Price vs. CC rematch brings great expectations. The two aces fought to a memorable draw in the first game, and now here they are a week later, getting ready to face each other again.

Both of them end up getting hit around a little bit this time, but Price does a little better job of not letting runners score, and our offense comes up big again in leading a 10–3 win with 47,646 watching.

Price absorbs the first blow when Marcus Thames homers off him in the second to put the Yankees up 2–0. Ben Zobrist drives home our first run with a single in the third, but he gets tagged out in a run-down play to end the inning. At that point, you have to kind of wonder whether we have let Sabathia off the hook when we could have gotten more. When you give someone like Sabathia a little wiggle room, more times than not he'll make you pay. When we mount threats in three of his first five innings and come away with nothing more, that line of thinking begins to spread throughout our team. Meanwhile, the Yankees add another run in the fifth to take a 3–1 lead. Fortunately, our offense isn't finished with Sabathia just yet.

Crawford opens the sixth with a single, and Longoria adds a double before an infield single by Rocco Baldelli scores Crawford from third.

After that, our offense tees off. Willy Aybar's RBI single ties the score before Sabathia walks his old battery mate from the Indians, Kelly Shoppach. That loads the bases for Sean Rodriguez, who walks to force in the go-ahead run.

Sabathia gets lifted with one out in the fifth, which is quite an accomplishment for our offense. The Yankees—and everybody in baseball—is used to seeing the big left-hander around in the late innings. They bring in Joba Chamberlain to face Upton, who hits a two-run double to deep center field. Crawford then adds a two-run single to finish off the seven-run sixth and give us an 8-3 lead.

We add two more in the seventh to build a seven-run cushion, and Mike Ekstrom, Jake McGee, and Andy Sonnanstine pitch the final three innings to seal the win.

Price allows three runs on eight hits in six innings to pick up his eighteenth win of the season. In the process, he shows a lot about what kind of pitcher he is. Any pitcher can go out there and pitch when he's got his good stuff, but you learn more about a pitcher when he doesn't have his best stuff. That's when he becomes a true pitcher. That's when he bears down to keep his team in the game as long as he can. And that's what Price did. In my opinion, he should be the American League Cy Young Award winner.

A lot of good things have happened in the finale against the Yankees, though we do suffer a setback during the seventh inning. Longoria fields a ground ball, and something looks odd when he flips the ball underhanded to second base to start an inning-ending double play. It turns out later that Longo aggravated his left quadriceps on the play. Joe gets him out of the game right away, and he's already being held out of the weekend games against the Mariners. We're going to need him back in the lineup to really be a dangerous club. Hopefully he'll feel better after the weekend.

Despite losing Longo for the weekend, we feel pretty good about leaving New York with a split, particularly after hitting one of the best lefties in the game pretty hard in the kind of atmosphere Yankee Stadium brings. We held our ground in this series.

By winning, we move back to within a half game of the Yankees. Boston hasn't played on this Thursday, so our magic number is reduced to four games.

Looking ahead, we finish our season with three games at Tropicana Field against Seattle, followed by a weekday three-game set against the Orioles to wrap up our home schedule. We'll then complete the season in Kansas City against the Royals with a four-game series.

The Yankees will host a three-game weekend series against the Red Sox, then they will travel to Toronto to play three against the Blue Jays. And on the final weekend of the season, they will play three against the Red Sox in Boston.

We finished with a 10–8 record against the Yankees this season, so if we finish the season tied with them for the top spot in the East, we will be the winners by virtue of the tiebreaker, which is head-to-head competition.

On paper we seem to have a clear advantage over the Yankees. Anyone would say our remaining road is easier. But we don't take anything for granted. I remember being on the other side of the equation when everybody saw the Devil Rays on the schedule and thought we'd be a pushover. Well, it's still the major leagues, and you'd better respect every team and take nothing for granted. When we look at our remaining schedule, we understand that we have a lot of work left to do if we want to realize our goal of winning the division.

Standings on September 23

Tm	W	L	GB
NYY	92	61	--
TBR	91	61	0.5
BOS	84	68	7.5
TOR	77	75	14.5
BAL	61	91	30.5

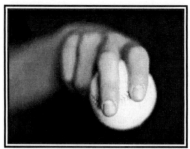

Four-seam fastball

NINE
September 24-26

TRAVEL IS ONE OF THE GRINDS of being a major-league baseball player. I know a lot of people would not understand that statement, and I'm well aware that our travel arrangements are of a grander nature than is typically the case for a business or family traveler, but the logistics of the traveling we do are demanding.

We usually leave for a road trip immediately after the final game of a series at Tropicana Field. We take a bus to the airport and fly in a charter, and you can't beat that part of it. Flying in a charter gives you all kinds of room to spread out, and you eat well, too. Most of the time, however, we're leaving after a night game, which gets us to our destination early the next morning for a game that night. We usually play for three days in a city, then leave for our next destination after the conclusion of the series.

In addition to the travel, there are the weird hours we have to keep. Sometimes those hours become extended like they did in New

York on the night of our rain delay. Usually we'll get to the park at around 2:00 in the afternoon and leave around midnight, but after the rain delay we got back to the hotel at around 1:30 A.M. The next day we still had to show up at two and get ready to play again in the final game of the series. The last game of the series was a 7:30 game, so we didn't get home to Tampa until 5 in the morning, and we then had to turn around and play Seattle that night.

Joe Maddon is really good about reducing the impact when the schedule bites us like that. He'll tell the team to come in later the next day, and he'll usually cancel batting practice to let us catch up on our rest. Staying fresh is important, because the energy with which you play the game can make the difference between winning and losing. Between the travel and the odd hours, keeping your energy up is a difficult proposition.

When I finally get out of bed on Friday, I notice that the Giants have defeated the Cubs 13–0 to take a half game lead over the Padres in the National League West. My cousin, Aaron Rowand, had a base hit in one at-bat.

I haven't been keeping in touch with him as much as I normally do, though we have been texting back and forth. I do know he hasn't been playing much. He signed a five-year deal with the Giants in 2008 and became the team's opening-day center fielder, but he's had a tough year, which all started after he got hit in the face by a Vincente Padilla pitch in April. He came away from that with a fractured cheek and a mild concussion that kept him on the disabled list for a couple of weeks. Aaron is a hard-nosed player who will run through a wall to catch a baseball, so I know he had to be hurting. Once he returned from the disabled list he never really got going, so his playing time has been reduced. Also contributing to his lack of playing time has been the play of Andres Torres and the team's acquisitions of Cody Ross and Pat Burrell.

I know a lot of Rays fans cringe at the mention of Burrell's name. He struggled with us after signing a big deal to become our designated hitter following the 2008 season. Fans look at the numbers, and Pat's were not the same for us as they had been when he played for Philadelphia. He just never seemed to get the hang of being a designated hitter, which is not the easiest thing to do if you're used to playing in the field. Pat had played in the field his whole career until he left the Phillies to join us as a free agent. The Rays finally released him on May 15.

A lot of people have criticized Pat. All I can say is that he was a consummate professional, and nobody worked harder than he did while he played for us. For some reason it just didn't work out. He's done pretty well with the Giants, though, which I'm happy to see.

I've also noticed that Aubrey Huff is keeping it loose on the Giants. He played for the Devil Rays when I came up with the team in 2006. He would do some funny stuff in the clubhouse, just like what I've read he's been doing with the Giants this season by employing a red thong that he's calling a "rally thong."

Apparently, Huffy began strutting around in the clubhouse before and after games while wearing a lacy red thong. He started the practice with 30 games remaining on this year's schedule and made the declaration that the "rally thong" would be worth at least 20 wins in the Giants' final 30 games. To Huff's way of thinking, 20 wins would lead the Giants to the National League West pennant.

For now, Huff's thong appears to have the Giants heading in the right direction. Maybe somebody on our team should start wearing a rally thong once we get to the playoffs. Nah, strike that. Not a good thought.

If the Giants can win their division and we can win ours, it would be awesome if we played each other in the World Series. Think how cool it would be for cousins to face off in the Fall Classic.

Aaron made the National League All-Star team when he played for the Phillies in 2007. That same year I was 6–0 in early June and appeared headed to the All-Star Game, which was played in San Francisco that season. I was hoping to make the team so we could play against each other, but I didn't make it. And by the time we faced the Phillies in the 2008 World Series, Aaron was gone. This time around I hope we see each other in the Series.

After playing the Yankees for four days, some might have expected us to not be all there Friday night when we play the Mariners in the first of three games at Tropicana Field. Fortunately for us, that isn't the case.

Jeff Niemann starts for us and seems to get back on track, which is good to see. Niems pitches 5 ⅔ innings to pick up his eleventh win of the season—the longest he has gone in a game since going on the disabled list with the shoulder problem.

Our 5–3 win coupled with a Yankees loss to the Red Sox puts us back into first place for the first time since September 16 and ties us with the Twins for the best record in the American League. Typifying the total team effort we've been getting all season, several notable things happen in the game.

Rafael Soriano sets a new single-season club record for saves by chalking up his forty-fourth of the season. He has converted each of his 22 save opportunities at home.

Sean Rodriguez starts at third, making him the second player in team history to start at seven different positions in one season. Ben Zobrist turned the trick during the 2009 season. On the bad side of that one, Longoria does not play, snapping his string of 102 consecutive games played.

In addition, Randy Choate pitches in his eightieth game of the season, extending his team record for appearances in a season.

And most important, we reduce our magic number for making the playoffs to three games.

Garza gets back on track in the second game of the series, holding the Mariners to one run on eight hits in seven innings to record his fifteenth win of the season in a 9–1 win. Meanwhile the Red Sox beat the Yankees again, so our win increases our lead to 1 ½ games while reducing our magic number to two games. That creates a scenario in which we could clinch a playoff spot if we win tomorrow and the Red Sox lose.

Taking the mound on Sunday afternoon in the series finale against the Mariners is exciting for me. I have a chance to start the game in which we clinch a playoff spot. In the back of my mind is a hope that I can pitch my first complete game of the season. I haven't gone the distance since 2008, which rubs me the wrong way. I feel like I should be doing that more often.

Unfortunately, I lay an egg, allowing five runs on eight hits in six innings to take my fourteenth loss of the season. And this loss probably stings more than any other this season because of my encounter with Josh Wilson.

I start the game with some of the best stuff I've had in a long time, which only adds to the frustration. My change is exactly where I want it to be, my curveball is good, and I locate my fastball the whole game. But a single pitch in the sixth inning of a 2–2 ballgame makes all the difference.

I know that I'll probably get taken out after the sixth because I'm approaching a hundred pitches. With runners on second and third and one out, I strike out Greg Halman for the second out to bring Wilson to the plate.

Josh played with us in 2007 and is not considered a home run threat, so I'm thinking, "Let's make a pitch here." I want to show him a fastball in, but I end up leaving it out over the plate. Wilson has had just one home run on the year. Go figure—one friggin' home run. I mean he used to play for us. I know the guy, and he's not a homer guy. But man, he squares up the fastball and powers that ball over the fence. That crushes me. Not only did I want to be on the mound when we clinched, I felt like I needed to start building some momentum by having some good outings going into the playoffs, and I was having a really good outing until this at-bat. Once again, the three-run home run has killed me. That's the thirty-fourth home run I've surrendered this season, which takes Tanyon Sturtze off the hook. The former Rays right-hander held the club record for most home runs in a season, but now that dubious distinction belongs to me.

One of my goals every season is to pitch 200 innings, and after this start I'm at 198 ⅓ innings heading into my final start of the season Friday night in Kansas City. Barring any unforeseen circumstances, that should give me my fourth consecutive year of reaching 200 or more innings in a season. I just like to get my job done and try to help us win games. Even if I don't get the decision in a game, if I can go deep enough into the game enough times every season, I'm helping the team by giving the bullpen a rest. If you do that all year, you're helping the bullpen stay fresh even in September, when we're trying to make a playoff push, rather than using them up at the beginning of the year. Starters make 34 or 35 starts a year, but if you're in the bullpen, you might pitch 70 to 80 times in a season and get up and down a lot in games you don't go into. When all is said and done, it's almost like the bullpen guys pitch every day.

One of the marvels of playing the Mariners is pitching against the great Ichiro Suzuki. That guy is unbelievable. I believe he's one of the greatest hitters of all time, if not *the* greatest hitter of all time. And the reason I'm saying that is that this guy came over to the major leagues from Japan at the age of 27, then posted ten straight seasons of 200 or more hits. Between playing in the United States and Japan, Ichiro has 3,500 total hits.

In Sunday's game he hits leadoff, and the thought enters my head that I want to move Jason Bartlett a couple of steps over to his right at shortstop. I want to throw Ichiro a fastball, and I know he likes to hit the ball in that direction. I look at Bartlett, kind of staring at him to see where he's at. I think to myself, "I'll throw this one pitch just off the plate, and he'll probably take it. Then I'll move Bartlett into the six-hole." So of course, Ichiro strokes my first-pitch fastball right through the hole where I was going to move Bartlett. After the inning I tell Bartlett, "I was going to move you over." We talk about it some more, and I say I want him to move toward the six-hole when I throw the fastball, and with an off-speed pitch, he can stay put or anticipate the ball getting hit up the middle. He knows what pitch is going to be thrown from watching the catcher's signals. But in Ichiro's next at-bat, Tom Foley, our third base/infield coach, moves Bartlett over to the six-hole right before I throw a changeup, and of course Ichiro hits it right up the middle. It's almost like this guy can place the ball wherever he wants. He's a totally different kind of hitter during the games than in batting practice. I know, because I watched him take batting practice yesterday, and he hit one bomb after another into the stands. Then all of a sudden, during the game, he's a little slap hitter, just getting his knocks. You've got to be one of the all-time greats to get ten straight seasons of 200 hits.

By losing on Sunday, we delay what now appears to be inevitable, which is clinching a spot in the playoffs for the second time in franchise history. The Red Sox lose to the Yankees, which cuts our magic number to one.

We're all pretty excited about clinching, but we're also anxious about finishing off this thing. Even though we haven't been playing that great lately, it's exciting to see our magic number go down and down. And having the Red Sox do a little number on the Yankees—winning two out of three over the weekend and almost winning Sunday night—is pretty exciting, because our main goal right now is to win the division. We know if we can win Monday night, we'll be in the playoffs no matter what. And even though we're not in the playoffs quite yet, we're already looking past that milestone to the idea of winning our second American League East title in three years. We want to be the best, which means having the best record in baseball, too. When we go out on the field, we want to win the game, but we are definitely scoreboard watching, too. I'm running back and forth to the clubhouse between innings to see who is winning the Yankees' game. This is exciting and it's what we play for. Having experienced this feeling in 2008, I know that it never gets old.

Standings on September 26

Tm	W	L	GB
TBR	93	62	--
NYY	93	63	0.5
BOS	86	69	7.0
TOR	80	75	13.0
BAL	61	94	32.0

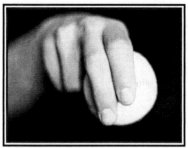

Cut fastball

TEN
September 27-29

YOU DEAL WITH A LOT OF THINGS on a ballclub together and individually.

Right now the team is dealing with Evan Longoria being out. We need him in our lineup, there's no doubt about that. He's a major force in the order. Without him, we have to come up with more innovative ways to score runs.

Lango's still listed as day-to-day, which is all about Joe Maddon wanting to avoid rushing him back too quickly in the regular season and risk not having him for the playoffs. Lango says that the injury feels better. He takes some ground balls and goes through some other drills prior to Monday night's game against the Orioles, but he isn't in the lineup for the game.

Individually, everyone deals with his own troubles. Carlos Pena has had a tough season.

Prior to Monday's game, Joe works with Carlos, employing some of his old hitting-coach pointers to give 'Los some things to think about in his approach. You can't ask for more from a teammate than you get from 'Los; he's the best. We all know he's working hard, and you can just feel his frustration. Actually, Joe might have been a contributor to Carlos's woes when he began using a shift against David Ortiz several years ago. That shift seemed to cool off Big Papi, and it also seemed to trigger the use of the shift by other teams. Carlos is a pull hitter, so hitting into that shift—where the second baseman moves into shallow right field and the shortstop moves over by second—has just killed Carlos's batting average. I'll bet that shift is responsible for shaving at least thirty points off his batting average, maybe more. He's still hitting home runs, but getting thrown out on that shift all the time will work on your head. Still, that's how Carlos leads. He never quits. He continues to work hard, and he's not too proud to accept help. All he's thinking about is helping the team.

The guys on the team are also aware of the pending decisions about which players will make up the playoff roster. Included in those decisions is which pitchers will make up the rotation in the first round.

Joe has continued to tell the media that 75 percent of the body of work is there, but that he still wants to go over some other information—including previous results against our as-yet-to-be-determined opponent—before making up his mind. He does tell the media prior to Monday night's game that he has talked to Andrew Friedman about the rotation and that "probably we know who the four guys are." But he notes, "Putting them in the right order is going to be the next part of it."

We all know that David Price will start the first game and that, if we've already clinched a playoff spot, he won't pitch Sunday in Kansas City—even if the outcome of that game will determine who wins our division. Price has 18 wins now, and if he picks up a win Tuesday night against Baltimore he'll have 19, leaving him one shy of 20 for the season. Nobody in Rays history has won 20, and now it appears Price won't get the chance to change that.

Not making a decision on the rotation and roster spots has led to some tension in the clubhouse, there's no doubt. Everybody wants to be on the postseason roster. More than likely we'll take four starters, and if they happen to go on a three-day rotation and decide to use Price on three days' rest, they'll probably throw that fourth starter into the bullpen. But there's definitely tension. There are guys coming up from Triple-A—like Jake McGee and Desmond Jennings—who haven't been on the team all year. But once the playoffs hit, it doesn't matter what you've done all year, it's about identifying the 25 players who will give you the best chance of going deep into the playoffs.

In some respects it puts a player in a weird position personally, because you think about yourself, but you also want what's best for the team. So you feel kind of guilty hoping you're going to have one of the spots no matter what. All you can do is try to pitch your butt off. There's no question, I'm thinking about it. I haven't pitched well enough to be a lock for that postseason roster, but, on the other hand, Joe knows I'm a competitor and that I have playoff experience. Hopefully I can contribute to our playoffs this year. But yeah, there's tension everywhere. I'm pitching right now and playing to make that postseason roster. I remember we didn't take Troy Percival and Edwin Jackson to the postseason in 2008, even though those two had done so much for us during the season. Management wasn't convinced that Troy was healthy enough to pitch for us, whereas Edwin, who had won 14 games for us, simply didn't make the cut. You just never know.

Despite all the anticipation, champagne does not touch our lips Monday night. We lose 4–0 to the Orioles, and the Red Sox continue their stubborn pursuit by beating the White Sox 6–1 in Chicago. You've got to tip your hat to the Red Sox. They are a professional group with a lot of pride. You have to respect the way they've played this season through all the adversity they've faced. As for the Orioles, they continue to be a pesky club. Aside from the disappointment of not clinching, we also fail to pick up a game on the Yankees on a night when they lose. Monday night's loss gives us our first back-to-back home losses since early August.

Brian Matusz pitches a nice game for Baltimore, holding our offense to no runs on three hits in seven innings while striking out eight. Matusz, who was the Orioles' top pick in the 2008 draft and the fourth selection overall, is a classy-looking left-hander with a nice variety of pitches. He commands all of those pitches, particularly his slider, and he continues to hit his spots throughout this game.

Wade Davis starts for us and matches Matusz zero for zero through four innings before Nick Markakis triples in the fifth to give the Orioles a 1–0 lead. The Orioles add three more in the seventh, and that's all they need given the way Matusz is pitching. Davis's loss snaps his seven-game winning streak.

I think everybody feels some frustration about not clinching, but we can't beat ourselves up about it. We'll just have to come back hard tomorrow night. Other frustrations stem from the sparse crowd at Tropicana Field tonight. After our loss, Longoria and Price step forth to express the team's disappointment that just 12,446 people have showed for a game in which we would have clinched a playoff spot with a win.

Longoria says the following:

"We've been playing great baseball all year. Since I've been here in '06, the fans have wanted a good baseball team. They have wanted to watch a contender. And for us to play good baseball for three years now and be in a spot to clinch again and go to the playoffs, I think it's just, we're all confused that there's only 15 or 20,000 in the building.

"I mean, we figured if we have a chance at the beginning of September, then maybe the fans will come. Now it's the end of September, almost October, and we're still kind of looking up at the seats and saying, 'Where is everybody?'"

Longo does not make a quick exit from the media. Instead he says he's been wanting to talk about the attendance for some time. He adds:

"I'm not trying to take a low blow at the fans, I'm just trying to rally the troops and get more people in here. I'm not trying to say that we have bad fans or any of that, because believe me, I've been here since '06 and I love the Tampa Bay community. It's just tough to see, and I feel like I was the right guy to say that."

Price, who is scheduled to pitch the second game of the series with Baltimore, tweets the following: "Had a chance to clinch a postseason spot tonight with about 10,000 fans in the stands. . . . Embarrassing."

In the aftermath of the comments by Longo and Price, the Rays announce that they will be giving away 20,000 free tickets to Wednesday night's regular-season home finale against the Orioles. Matt Silverman, the team president, notes:

"You heard from a couple of our players about the crowd last night. You can sense from that and other comments throughout the year that our players really thrive on the energy in the ballpark when it's full of our fans. We have a very good record in this ballpark on Saturday night concerts and other games where we're able to pack the place in."

I like what Longo and Price did. I think the cities of St. Petersburg and Tampa have to understand that we just want to get the fans out here, and we need them. They really help us. Longo and Price didn't mean any harm. They weren't trying to degrade the area. We understand that during the season fans can't always attend the games, and we know these are tough economic times, particularly in the Tampa Bay region. But we only have one week left in the season and we're a playoff-bound team. We're in first place in the American League East and we need their support. I think that's where Longo and Price were coming from.

Price calls me the next morning, saying, "I'm so screwed. The fans are going to boo me so bad." He's very worried about the reaction to his tweet. He didn't mean for it to come out the way it did. He got a lot of bad feedback when he said it, and now he feels terrible. I tell him that he needs to focus on his pitching and not worry about the fans.

We need a win Tuesday night, and Price does what he needs to, like a true No. 1 starter.

For eight innings, he dominates the Orioles. Rafael Soriano then gets the final three outs, giving us a 5–0 win and officially putting us into the playoffs for the second time in the history of the franchise. The Yankees also clinch a spot in the postseason, but we're still ahead of them by a half game in the division race. Our magic number to clinch the East is now four games. We have five games left and the Yankees have four.

Price looks overpowering as only Price can look, striking out eight and walking none. He says later that on the heels of his little tweet about the fans, he felt like he had to throw nine innings or be toast.

After the game, he tells the media, "We want more fans here, obviously. We love our fans that come; that's not what I was saying last night, obviously, but that was a nightmare last night."

B.J. Upton gets our offense going with an RBI single in the second. Crawford then shows his speed in the third when he scores from first base on Dan Johnson's double into the right-field corner. That gives C.C. 105 runs scored this season, breaking the Rays' record of 104 that he set in 2004. No one doubts that he'll score more runs before the season ends, so the new record will keep going up.

Carlos Pena hits a solo home run in the fourth, giving him his first homer since September 14 while giving us a 3–0 lead. Ben Zobrist then adds a sacrifice fly, and C.C. homers in the fifth to make it 5–0. That offensive spurt, though greatly appreciated, really isn't needed given the way Price pitches, but you never know. That performance by Price speaks volumes about what kind of a money pitcher he is. Look at all the pressure he put on himself and how he responded to that pressure—pretty amazing.

While we win Tuesday night, we all understand that we have more goals to accomplish this season, like winning the division, grabbing the best record, then balling out in the postseason. But that does not stop us from enjoying the moment.

Our celebration turns out to be even more fun than our four celebrations in 2008: the one when we clinched a playoff berth, the one when we won our division, another after we beat the White Sox in the Division Series, and finally, the monster of a celebration we enjoyed when we beat the Red Sox to advance to the World Series.

When Price finishes the eighth inning with the game in hand, we know that Joe will put Soriano into the game and that the game is essentially over. I feel good about the way everything has played out. Soriano *should* be out there at the end. I think he told Joe that he wanted to finish the game, he wanted to be the guy to get the final outs to send us into the playoffs. To me that shows a lot of heart. Price and Soriano are the only guys who should be out there pitching on the night we clinch. Those two are the MVPs of our staff this year.

As we watch the final inning, I begin talking to Jennings, who has never experienced what we're about to experience. That gets me all excited to celebrate. Once Adam Jones strikes out swinging, we all bolt onto the field and the crowd goes nuts. We have a great crowd tonight, and they're so loud it's unbelievable.

Champagne bottles are everywhere when we get back to the clubhouse. Visqueen plastic sheeting is taped everywhere to cover our lockers and the carpet. We're outfitted with Oakley goggles to protect our eyes, and we basically start going crazy. Clinching is such a relief. You've worked so hard all year to get to this point, and it feels good to just let it all go. You never know if the next celebration is going to be your last, so you have to do it up right whenever you get a chance.

After quickly getting soaked inside the clubhouse, we take the celebration onto the field to show the fans how much we appreciate them showing up. We got a lot of support from the fans who showed up tonight and all season. You should always appreciate the fans and never forget them, because they are the reason we have jobs. We play for the city, the fans, and ourselves. We charge around, spraying the fans with champagne, and they love it. Tropicana Field feels like one giant party.

Garza cracks me up. That guy is all over the place, spraying every single person he sees. When he gets back into the clubhouse he starts dousing guys with entire buckets of cold water. When he splashes B.J. with one, B.J. screams like a little girl in this high-pitched voice, and it's hilarious—B.J. catches a lot of crap for that. When the celebration airs on TV, they bleep out the f-bombs.

We get into the cigar stash in Joe's office and start lighting up. Yes, Tropicana Field is a smoke-free building, and most of us don't like cigars, but hey, you don't make the playoffs every day. We haven't allowed wives and kids into the celebration this year, so we hang out some in the food room, smoke our cigars, and keep downing or spraying our champagne. We started with 200 bottles of the bubbly and no telling how many cases of beer.

Since the game ended around 9 o'clock, the party draws to a close pretty early. We have limos to take care of us tonight, and everyone has left their cars at their houses, so the celebration continues in the limos that take us home. I ride in one with Wade Davis, Garza, Sean Rodriguez, Jake McGee, and Kelly Shoppach, and some of us have our wives crammed in there, too. Of all places, we end up at a McDonald's on Ulmerton Road. We pile out of the limo and head inside, where we buy cheeseburgers, Chicken McNuggets, and what seems like everything else on the menu. I laugh to myself, thinking that we've just clinched a spot in the postseason and we're celebrating at McDonald's, but we have a blast. People ordering at the drive-through recognize us and get all excited. They're congratulating us and telling us to go all the way. We end up staying out until about 3:30 in the morning.

After all that, I somehow feel pretty good the next morning. I'm not really hung over. I guess the secret is to throw more beer and champagne than you drink. I learned that trick in 2008.

I wake up around 7:30 to take my daughter to school. Though not hung over, I'm certainly tired, so I'm sure it's not the most pleasant wake-up call for her. While she gets ready, I prepare her lunch.

Normally my daughter's lunch is composed of really healthy stuff, but not the day after clinching a playoff spot. I say, "This is your lucky day," and fix her a Nutella (hazelnut spread) sandwich. I pack Gummy Bears, chocolate cookies, and chips. I really don't know what I'm doing, but I figure that since we got to celebrate, she deserves to celebrate, too.

After I drop her off at school, I take care of my six-month-old and let my wife sleep in until about noon. Then it's time for me to go to the park, work out, and do my thing.

When I get to the park I think for a moment that I must be late, because the fans are already lined up around the building to wait their turn to cash in on the free-ticket offer by our ownership. Like I said, we might not have the biggest turnout every night, but we have some loyal fans. They wait in sweltering heat, and they keep waiting when the heat turns to rain. By the time the doors open, we have a sellout crowd of 36,973 inside the building to watch our final regular-season home game.

Unfortunately, we go out with a 2–0 loss.

Kevin Millwood turns in a vintage performance for Baltimore, evoking memories of when he was considered one of the best right-handers in baseball. I enjoy watching a guy like him pitch. A veteran who once had dominating stuff, Millwood carries into his start against us a 3–16 record with a 5.29 ERA, which is hardly representative of what he has done during his 14 years in the major leagues. He manages to turn back the clock against us, relying more on his pitching knowledge than physical ability. Everything he throws our guys seems to be on the corner—changeups, backdoor breaking balls, and sliders—and he manages to keep us off balance. Obviously he doesn't have the same stuff that he used to have, but he's a lot smarter. He seems to be two steps ahead of the hitters all night.

The only chance we have against him comes in the seventh. Zobrist draws a leadoff walk, and Crawford singles to center field. Dan Johnson's groundout moves the runners into scoring position for Pena, but Millwood gets Carlos on a shallow fly ball to center. That brings Joyce to the plate, and Joyce watches three balls go past to put him ahead in the count, 3–0. At that point, Millwood elects to walk Joyce intentionally rather than risk grooving him one, and that strategy pays off when he strikes out B.J. for the third out to escape the jam.

Even though we lose, we manage to reduce our magic number to clinch the American League East to three games, since the Yankees lose to the Blue Jays 8–4.

Nieman takes the loss, but he's starting to resemble his old self. Baltimore can't do anything against him until they get two runs in the seventh, and that's all they need given the way Millwood pitches.

We finish with a 49–32 mark at home. After the game, we head to Kansas City, where we're scheduled to begin a four-game series against the Royals on Thursday night. Meanwhile, the Yankees have to travel to Boston to begin a three-game series against the Red Sox Friday night.

You never want to look too far ahead, but we like our chances of winning the division.

Standings on September 29

Tm	W	L	GB
TBR	94	64	--
NYY	94	65	0.5
BOS	87	71	7.0
TOR	82	76	12.0
BAL	63	95	31.0

Changeup

Eleven

September 30—
October 2

Winning the division, no matter what our schedule shows, is beginning to look more and more difficult.

Kansas City plays us like they don't want a drop of champagne spilled in the visiting clubhouse.

Matt Garza starts the opening game of the series on Thursday night, and we end September on a losing note.

Garza has a quality start, allowing just three runs on five hits in seven innings. But Garza isn't the problem, Zach Greinke is. All he gives up in seven innings is a solo homer to Carl Crawford and a sacrifice fly to Reid Brignac while scattering four hits and striking out nine in a 3–2 Royals win.

Garza breaks the 200-innings mark while taking his tenth loss.

Since the Yankees don't play, we go to bed Thursday night tied with them once again.

Prior to Friday night's game we have a team meeting. Joe Maddon just wants to let us know that he thinks we've looked like a bunch of tight asses the last few games, and he tells us that we aren't that kind of team. Instead we're a team that's loose—we laugh, we smile, we have fun, and it seems like we have a mixture of every cartoon character imaginable among us. Joe tells us he doesn't care if we're in a pennant race or in the playoffs, we should go out there and have fun. And while we're out there having fun, he wants us to enjoy ourselves and carry confidence and a swagger with us.

Guys from other teams are always asking me about all the fun we have in the dugout. It's evident to other teams. After this meeting, I think we all realize how much pressure we've been putting on ourselves lately. We just need to relax a little and enjoy the moment.

I'm all about enjoying the moment, but I'm not that big on changing my routine. Even though this has been a difficult season for me personally, I have not wavered from my routine prior to the start of a game in which I'm pitching. When I go into the trainer's room to get stretched out, I always listen to the same song, "Bro Hymn," by Pennywise. I've listened to that as far back as the minor leagues. That song just pumps me up.

While some might suggest that I should change my routine because the results haven't been that great this season, I'm not big on that idea. As a player, you try to stay as consistent as you can. You try not to change too many things. You'll change your mechanics. You'll change your thought process. You'll change a lot of things. But there are some things you need to keep the same. That's what consistency is all about. I might change my cleats or glove, but there are some things I just don't change. I also write the numbers 25 and 44 on the back of the mound before the first inning I pitch. I've done that for a long time. One of my really good buddies that I played baseball with in high school, Nolan Lemar, died in a car accident, and the number he wore on his uniform was 25. The No. 44 is for my best friend Josh's father, Bill Edwards, who died of cancer. That's the number he wore when he played football.

Going into my final start of the season on Friday night, I'm a little disappointed that we lost yesterday. Had we won last night and tonight, and were the Yankees to lose to the Red Sox tonight, we could have clinched the division tonight.

Alas, things rarely turn out the way you see them turning out in your mind.

One of the difficulties of facing a team like Kansas City is that we don't play them often. They have a bunch of young guys I'm not familiar with, other than from reading scouting reports and watching video. Going up against a group of free-swinging kids without a lot of experience can go either way, though I like my chances.

I know the Royals can hit pretty well. That's one element of the game they've been consistent with all season. Last night's loss in the opener tells me they aren't one of those teams that's just trying to get the season over with; rather, they're trying to end the season strong.

You can think about that kind of stuff, but it doesn't help what you're trying to do out there on the mound. Even though my numbers don't look so hot, I feel like I've been pitching pretty well. I have to go out there, do my thing, and pitch the way I know how. I've been feeling good in the bullpen, and I want to end my season on a strong note. If I execute my pitches, I can achieve that goal.

Figuring that the Royals will be aggressive at the plate, I want to be smart with my pitch selection. I want to change up a few things by throwing more fastballs in off-speed counts and more off-speed pitches in fastball counts. I've been in a little rut, throwing too many changeups on two-strike counts, and hitters have adjusted accordingly, looking for the changeup with two strikes.

My changeup is a tough pitch to figure out the first time you see me, so I feel like I have a big advantage going into the game against hitters who haven't faced me. Then again, I've had my share of buzzard's luck in September, and I'm well aware that sometimes, when you face a young team like the Royals, they hack away with no fear. If they're looking for changeups with two strikes and get fastballs instead, I can have a good night. So I decide to throw more two-strike fastballs.

When I take the mound in Kansas City, the calendar says October 1, and September is in my rearview mirror. Sadly, the new month does not bring a different outcome.

The game has a strange beginning. We appear to turn a triple play in the first inning, but the home-plate umpire blows the call at the plate that would have completed the play, and the Royals come out of the first with a 1–0 lead. I feel like I have good stuff, especially with my curveball, but I miss locations on a couple of fastballs and pay for it when they get me for a two-spot in the third to take a 3–0 lead.

I've left the ball up again at the wrong times, which continues to happen because of the mechanical flaw I've identified but haven't been able to correct over the entire second half of the season. Also, I'm not bearing down and making my pitch in a couple of situations when I need to do so. There are only a couple of guys in their lineup that I know—I haven't seen a lot of these guys—but that seems to make things tougher rather than easier. They're just hacking at everything, and they're tough to figure out.

The eventual bottom line is a whopping seven runs on twelve hits in five innings. Given the way my season has gone, such an ending seems appropriate. There is nothing I can do about it right now. I just have to look forward to the playoffs and hope that I'm on the playoff roster.

My pitching isn't the team's only concern. You do have to score occasionally to win games, and the offense, minus Evan Longoria, is having a hard time scoring. Lango did not play again tonight, and we really could have used a quality right-handed bat against their starting pitcher, left-hander Bruce Chen.

Not having Lango definitely hurts us, not only on offense but on defense, too. You really notice he's missing after a few games, because everything involving the third baseman is just a little bit slower than normal or the range just an inch off here or there. He's such a big factor in any game we play. He wanted to play tonight, but the team has decided to continue resting him until the playoffs.

Chen pitched great, allowing just two hits while going the distance for a complete-game shutout.

The Yankees got rained out in Boston, so that leaves us a half game out of first place when we go to bed Friday night.

On Saturday afternoon, the clubhouse seems to be as loose as it normally is before a night game, particularly during the college football season. Everybody has a favorite team, and the crap everybody takes is usually dictated by their allegiance to their favorite team.

Even though I'm from California, I pull for LSU because I almost went there on a baseball scholarship. Within the clubhouse, that makes Reid Brignac and me tight on Saturdays, since he's from Baton Rouge and grew up an LSU fan. Randy Choate is an FSU guy, having gone to college there, and B.J. Upton is right there with him because he had signed a baseball scholarship to play for the 'Noles before signing with the Devil Rays, who selected him with the second pick of the 2002 June draft. Lance Cormier is probably the biggest college football fan on our team. He's all about the University of Alabama, where he played college baseball, and he follows the Crimson Tide with religious fervor. Last year he won a big bet with Chris Westmoreland, our equipment and home clubhouse manager, on the outcome of the SEC Championship Game between Alabama and Westy's beloved University of Florida. Alabama won the game, and the payoff came during spring training this year when Westy had to parade around the clubhouse wearing Alabama gear all spring. So everybody is kind of tuned in to the outcome of the Alabama-Florida game on Saturday. Alabama is going into the game ranked No. 1, and Florida is No. 7.

Reid and I begin catching a bunch of crap when Tennessee stops LSU on a botched play near the end zone, which appears to end the game. Only Tennessee had too many players on the field, so LSU gets another chance and ends up scoring to win 16–14.

The Alabama-Florida game has not yet started when we leave the clubhouse, but everybody remains interested in the outcome of that one.

Saturday brings more thoughts to me about the coming announcement of the playoff roster, but the day brings no resolution as to who will be on it. The last time we went to the playoffs, I knew where I'd be. I was pitching better than anybody else on the team, so I knew I would start the first game of our Division series against the White Sox.

Obviously, this year has felt a little different, since I've been struggling all year long. I've had some great games and some really bad ones. But if you take out three of my worst outings, I would be carrying an ERA under 4.00 instead of over 5.00. One positive from last night's start is that I met one of my season's goals by surpassing the 200-inning mark for the fourth consecutive year. That means a lot to me.

While I've reached some goals that I'm happy with, waiting to find out if I'll be pitching in the postseason continues to be nerveracking. It's stupid when you think about it, because I've pitched my last game of the regular season, so the decision is out of my hands. Nevertheless, I'll continue to have a lot of anxiety until the decision is made.

Despite my record, I think I should be on the playoff roster due to my experience and what I've done.

It looks like Minnesota will be playing the Wild Card team, so the question of which opponent we want to play continues to float around the clubhouse. I like the idea of playing Minnesota, even if they have home-field advantage in a best-of-five series. The Twins play at Target Field, which is a nice, spacious ballpark. The ball seems to fly out of the park in Texas, one of the reasons, of course, being that they have the hitters to put the ball in the stands— hitters like Josh Hamilton, Nelson Cruz, Ian Kinsler, and Michael Young, to name a few.

Some guys are still questioning whether the Yankees are really busting it to win the division, since a matchup with the Twins looks so much more favorable, even if they would have to play three in Minnesota. But there is no way anybody can answer the question about the Yankees' intent.

After Friday night's rainout in Boston, the Yankees have to play a double-header against the Red Sox on Saturday.

Performing poorly this season has made me grow some thick skin. I've been caught a little off guard by some of the things that have been written and said about me. It sucks getting scrutinized and torn town. You know, I've never had to deal with the media getting personal on me like that before. You treat the media as well as you can, then you realize how quickly it can turn. When the media starts criticizing you, people are blogging about you, and fans don't want you on the team anymore, it kind of sets you back a little bit. No matter what you do or say, it's all about whether you perform. It's just a part of the game, and I know that. It's been going on for a hundred years. But like my dad always told me, "If you don't like it, pitch better." So although it might be a part of the game I don't like, it is still a part of the game, and I have to wear it.

Andy Sonnanstine starts Saturday night's game, and we use a bunch of relievers by design. Sonnie pitches 2 $\frac{1}{3}$ innings and is followed by Chad Qualls, who gets two outs. Then a parade follows that includes Jeremy Hellickson, David Price, Jake McGee, Grant Balfour, Joaquin Benoit, and Choate. That group gets the job done, and we beat the Royals 4–0.

It turns out that we establish an odd record in this game. Eight pitchers is the most ever used in a major-league game by a team going to the playoffs. Odd, but we'll take it.

Meanwhile, C.C. hits another home run and Joyce has a two-run triple to feed the offense.

Inside the clubhouse after the game, Westy takes a lot of abuse when Florida gets smoked by Alabama, 31–6. Cormier probably says "Roll Tide" a hundred times if he says it once.

Most importantly, the Yankees split with the Red Sox, which whittles down our magic number to one game. If the Red Sox beat the Yankees on Sunday we win. If the Yankees beat the Red Sox on Sunday and we beat the Royals, we win—because we hold the tiebreaker. Our only chance of not winning the division comes down to us losing and the Yankees winning. In other words, we control our own destiny heading into the final day of the season. That's what a pennant race is supposed to be all about.

Standings on October 2

Tm	W	L	GB
TBR	95	66	--
NYY	95	66	--
BOS	88	73	7.0
TOR	84	77	11.0
BAL	66	95	29.0

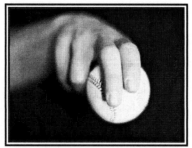

Two-seam fastball

TWELVE
October 3

Back on May 23, when we had our biggest lead in our division, we knew not to get too happy. Knowing how much talent resides in the American League East makes such a stance easy. We knew there was no use in dreaming about running away with the division, even if we did have a six-game lead. Joe Maddon said then that the winner of the division would be determined on the final day of the season, and he repeated that message many times during the course of the summer.

Well, Joe was right. On October 3, the final day of the season, the winner of the 2010 American League East crown will be determined. We want to be that team. Everybody in the clubhouse knows that a lot of guys on the team will be elsewhere in 2011. We want to make one last run. I mean, no matter if you go to the World Series or not, you still want to be the American League East champions. That's our goal, and if we achieve it, no matter what happens during the playoffs, we will at least have something memorable from the season to hang our hats on.

I know everybody is thinking about that at some point on Sunday morning. We have a special group, and nobody wants to see the group break up. But we're all guys, so that kind of stuff normally gets internalized. If you were to walk into the clubhouse, you would think it's a typical Sunday morning.

Everybody is lying around on the couches with their iPads figuring out their fantasy football lineups and talking trash. Everybody is doing their thing. It just seems like a normal day. Nobody is pressing too much or hurrying to get ready. I measure the hair from my Afro—4 ½ inches on the final day of the season.

Since division play began in 1969, this is the eighth time that two teams from the same division have entered the final day in a tie for the lead.

The Yankees game starts before ours, which elevates scoreboard watching to an artform.

Throughout the game, guys are running back to the clubhouse to check on the Yankees score, then returning to the dugout with a full report. We know that the Red Sox take a 2–0 lead on a two-run homer by J.D. Drew, but then we learn that Nick Swisher has homered for the Yankees in the second and Alex Rodriguez has driven home another in the third to tie the score.

On the field, we come out kind of flat, lacking the energy we need for this kind of game. We're just kind of plugging along. Wade Davis pitches well, but the offense is stymied against a right-hander named Sean O'Sullivan.

Davis pitches seven innings and has a fairly clean line—three hits, two walks, and six strikeouts. But Alex Gordon hits a two-run homer in the fourth that gives the Royals a 2–0 lead.

O'Sullivan pitches well, holding us to no runs on two hits in six innings. Then Robinson Tejeda and Gil Meche add scoreless frames to take us to the ninth inning trailing 2–0.

At approximately 3:47 central standard time, David Price returns to the dugout from a trip to the clubhouse yelling, "We won. We're the champs of the AL East." The Red Sox have finished off the Yankees 8–4. We're all excited, jumping up and down, which must look pretty weird to the Royals. Here we are celebrating in the dugout and we still have a game going on. All the guys in the field are looking in and clapping, and it's kind of a strange moment.

While we know now that we're the champions of the American League East, we still have that 2–0 deficit staring us in the face, and we'd like to win the division on the field and not have the Red Sox do the job for us. It's more nerve-racking when you're sitting on the bench watching than when you're pitching, because you have no control over anything, so I watch nervously as we seem to find some reserve of energy and begin to really focus on winning the game.

Joakim Soria enters the game to pitch the ninth, bringing along an impressive body of work. The Royals closer has not suffered a blown save since May 6, and he has not allowed a run since July 28 against the Twins.

Carl Crawford opens the inning with an infield single, but before we can get too happy about that, Dan Johnson looks at a called third strike, which furthers the odds against us. Soria has been nasty all year, and he doesn't look any different against us. Matt Joyce then pokes a single through the middle to bring to the plate Carlos Pena, our leader and the soul of the team. I hope he can deliver some magic. If anyone deserves a break, Carlos is the guy.

And he delivers. Appropriately, he goes the other way, stroking a double to left to drive home C.C. and Joyce and tie the game.

Normally, the last thing any team wants to do is go to extra innings on a getaway day, but this time around we don't mind that a bit.

In the tenth and eleventh innings, we go down in order.

Jeff Niemann pitches the bottom of the eleventh for us and strikes out the side. Afterwards he's really pumped up about it, as well he should be. He went in with the game on the line in extra innings and just mowed them down. Three strikeouts. That's the nastiest I've ever seen him pitch.

I think the team gets a lift from Niems' performance, and that carries over into our next turn at bat.

Joe puts Rocco Baldelli in to pinch hit to lead off the twelfth, and he lines a single into left and then steals second base. Two outs later, Kelly Shoppach hits a shot to third off Greg Holland that Wilson Betemit boots, and Rocco races home with the go-ahead run. Rafael Soriano then enters the game. With two outs, Gregor Blanco doubles, which makes for some final suspense, but Soriano then strikes out Mike Aviles swinging to preserve the win and earn his forty-fifth save of the season.

Our 3–2 win gives us a 96–66 record for the season, the best record in the American League. We not only earn the division title but get home-field advantage throughout the playoffs. One hour and 2 minutes after receiving the news about the Yankees' loss, we have claimed our second American League East title in three years and have accomplished that feat in the manner that we wanted. Having one more win than the Yankees seems to validate everything. We knew we owned the tiebreaker against the Yankees, but we wanted to have the better record. Team has always been the top priority for this group. We have a nice chemistry, and all of us care about the club. Now we need eleven more wins to achieve our ultimate goal, which is to win a World Series.

Winning the game on Sunday makes for a totally different kind of celebration, bittersweet in some respects. Through the mist of champagne spraying around the room, I look at all the smiles and wonder if this will be the final time C.C., 'Los, Garz, Balfour, or any number of the guys inside our clubhouse will be celebrating together. The window was closing, and we answered the challenge and got it done. That feels pretty good at the moment. So I soak it all in, and the feeling couldn't be better.

Standings on October 3

Tm	W	L	GB
TBR	96	66	--
NYY	95	67	1.0
BOS	89	73	7.0
TOR	85	77	11.0
BAL	66	96	30.0

EPILOGUE

The 2010 Playoffs and 2011

COMING OUT ON TOP in the tough American League East brought a special feeling to our group in 2010.

To play in the Tampa Bay market and beat out New York, Boston, Toronto, and Baltimore, with the players those teams have, was particularly rewarding. I think what we accomplished by winning our second division title in three years spoke to the talent we had and to our creative front office. The Rays are a little bit old-school in the way they operate, growing their own talent and augmenting that talent with selective acquisitions along the way.

While we won the division, we weren't playing our best baseball at the end of the season. We went 13–14 in September before finishing at 2–1 in October. We didn't exactly have a dazzling final month, and individually, I don't think it could have gone much worse for me. I felt great, but I wasn't pitching well. I had been fighting myself the entire season and didn't win a game that last month. That was disappointing. I felt like I should have contributed more during the stretch drive.

When a team doesn't play the kind of baseball in the final month that it has played all year, it's tough to get that chemistry reignited in the postseason.

The best record in the American League earned us a spot in the playoffs against the Rangers. Had we advanced, we would have had the home-field advantage in the American League Championship Series as well.

Meanwhile, some speculated that the Yankees got what they wanted, facing the Twins in the Division Series—as if they somehow tanked the division race in order to play the Twins and avoid facing Cliff Lee in a best-of-five series in the first round of the playoffs. I didn't believe any of that then and still don't. Like us, the Yankees failed to finish the season on a high note. They went 12–15 in September before going 1–2 in October. You can talk all you want about wanting to rest your pitchers and your players, but you'd much rather be playing good baseball going into the playoffs, and neither the Yankees nor we were doing so.

I didn't find out until the Monday after our weekend series in Kansas City that I would be on the playoff roster and would start Game 2. Jim Hickey told Matt Garza and me the news when we were throwing our bullpens. I think the reason they took so long to decide was that they wanted to be sure of our opponent before establishing the rotation. Minnesota was a different team than the Rangers.

Given my body of work for the organization over the past four years, I had a pretty good idea that I'd be starting. Still, I'd had a little hiccup in 2010, and not until I heard the news on Monday was I certain.

Joe noted that my home/road splits were a factor in his decision to start me in Game 2. He told the media, "Without giving up all of our inner secrets, I'm sure you could look through all the statistical information and try to glean why we would do it."

Sorting through the data, I had a better ERA at Tropicana Field, and I had pitched decently against the Rangers during the season, going 1–1 with a 2.57 ERA in two starts.

Getting picked to be on the roster made me want to smile, but I couldn't show too much excitement in the clubhouse, because a lot of my teammates were feeling the pain of exclusion.

That whole situation isn't easy on anybody. In fact, it's unbelievably awkward, almost (but not quite) as bad as when somebody gets released. Players simply have to learn how to deal with that stuff. You say, "Hey man, you pitched your ass off for us all year long. You definitely deserve to be on the roster. But even if you're not, we need you here. We need that support."

I had decided ahead of time that if I didn't make the roster, I would be disappointed, but I planned on being there for the team.

We headed into the playoffs to face the Rangers, who had won six of their final ten games. While that's not exactly red hot, it was a better end to the season than ours, and they were able to roll out Cliff Lee in the opener at Tropicana Field. David Price started for us, and they just got after us.

Lee allowed only a solo home run to Ben Zobrist during his seven-inning stint, and the Rangers took the opener 5–1. The next night I started for us, and C.J. Wilson threw 6 $\frac{1}{3}$ scoreless innings against us to lead a 6–0 Rangers win, putting us down 0–2 as we headed to Texas for games three and four.

I don't think I pitched badly in my start. There is no feeling like the playoffs. Walking onto the field, you get chills down your spine. Pitching in the playoffs is not the same as pitching in the regular season. You know that not only are the people in the stands watching you, everyone is watching because yours is the only baseball game in the world being broadcast at that time. So it's a totally different, much larger stage.

I gave up two runs in the first four innings, and in the top of the fifth, I hit Matt Treanor to start the inning. One out later Elvis Andrus hit a single, and that's when Joe came out of the dugout to get me. I was pretty surprised. I'd only thrown 68 pitches. But that's the manager's call. Chad Qualls took my place and Michael Young greeted him with a home run to center field. That put the Rangers up 5–0 and pretty much sealed our fate.

We managed to win two in Texas to force a Game 5 at Tropicana Field to see which team would advance to the American League Championship Series. Once again they wheeled out Lee, and this time he pitched a complete game, allowing one run on six hits while striking out thirteen. The visiting team won every game of the series, which is pretty weird.

We felt like we could have won that series, but I don't think we played the baseball we wanted to. And just like that, our season was over.

Bummed out about the abrupt end, I braced myself for the coming off-season. I knew a lot of guys would not be back, and I wondered if I would be one of those headed elsewhere. Baseball is a crazy game. A lot of what happens is business. I had met some goals that I wanted to meet, but I didn't have the year I wanted to have. I hoped I would not be getting traded and that I could get back to work and improve myself for 2011.

Texas ended up beating the Yankees in six games to advance to the World Series, where they lost to the Giants in five games. It appeared that the magic of Aubrey Huff's thong carried through like he said it would. I was happy for my cousin Aaron. I just wished we could have been there in the World Series, playing against them.

After a little time off, I got back to work. I wanted to be in the best shape of my career in 2011, and I wanted to have my mechanical issues ironed out so that I wouldn't have to think about my mechanics when I went to the mound. If I was going to be back with the Rays in 2011, I had to do my part.

Pretty soon the departures began.

Carl Crawford signed a seven-year, $142 million deal to play with the Red Sox. The only surprise about that one was that he went to the Sox. I kind of thought he'd be going to the Angels. But I was happy for him. Carlos Pena signed a one-year, $10 million deal to go to the Cubs. And that's how it went. Dan Wheeler went to the Red Sox, Randy Choate to the Marlins, Grant Balfour to the Athletics, Joaquin Benoit to the Tigers, and Rafael Soriano to the Yankees. We also made two trades. One sent Jason Bartlett to the Padres, a trade rooted in the belief that Reid Brignac would be able to step in at shortstop and fill Bartlett's shoes. And Garza got traded to the Cubs.

None of the news really shocked me except for the Garza trade. I knew Crawford was going to go, and I had a feeling Pena was going to go. Bartlett's departure was foreseeable given Brignac's progress. Grant Balfour had talked to me, and although he really wanted to come back, he also wanted a multi-year deal, so it was no great surprise when he ended up going somewhere else. Soriano, I knew, was going to be gone. I wish all of them could have stayed. We had such a great team last year.

Everybody wrote us off at the start of the 2011 season.

We have a new bullpen and different faces on the field, but we're still in the hunt heading into the final week of August. Though we're in third place, we're within striking distance of the Yankees and Red Sox. We're almost exactly where the Red Sox were a year ago, and once again the same three teams are duking it out for the division title and A.L. Wild Card. Maybe we're not just hunting the Beasts of the East anymore. Maybe we're one of them.

Like Joe Maddon says, until we're mathematically eliminated, we're not eliminated. Once again, September nights are going to be exciting.

And as for me, I got off to one of the best starts of my career this year. At one point I pitched three successive complete games, and I have eight complete games so far in 2011. Finishing what I start was one of my goals for this year after going two seasons without a complete game. It feels really good to experience the positive results of all the hard work I did during the offseason. I'm thrilled that I made the All-Star team for the first time in my career, too.

I start making bigger money next season. I'm hoping the Rays will keep me in the fold anyway, but you never know. You can always wake up tomorrow and be headed elsewhere. That's just baseball. If you can stick with the same team your whole career, you're the exception. I'd love to stay with Tampa Bay my whole career. I love it here. But that's part of it. It's just the way the game works. Sometimes other teams need pitching, or other teams need offense or outfielders, and they go out and get them.

While I have new teammates in 2011 and we're still managing to win games, I won't soon forget the team we had in 2010. I'll remember that group for having the best chemistry in the big leagues. We had a lot of talent, but talent can only take you so far. It gets you some wins and some big knocks, but if you have good team chemistry you are going to play consistently good baseball, and that's how you win a division.

The window of opportunity we had in 2010 has closed. But like they say, baseball imitates life, and you soon discover in baseball, as in life, that when one window closes, another one opens.

JAMES SHIELDS was born and raised in the Los Angeles area of California. The Tampa Bay Devil Rays drafted him in the sixteenth round of the 2000 June draft, and he reached the major leagues in 2006. Since then, Shields has been one of the main cogs in Tampa Bay's pitching rotation and has been an American League All-Star. He resides in Clearwater, Florida.

BILL CHASTAIN attended Georgia Tech and covered the Rays for the *Tampa Tribune* prior to covering the team for MLB.com. Chastain has penned other books, including *Payne at Pinehurst, Steel Dynasty, Peachtree Corvette Club, The Streak* and *Hack's 191* (due out in January 2012). He lives in Tampa, Florida.